Touchstones 2

A TEACHING ANTHOLOGY
Revised and expanded edition

MICHAEL AND PETER BENTON

Hodder & Stoughton

LONDON SYDNEY AUCKLAND

ISBN 0 340 39412 9

First published 1969
Second edition 1972
Third edition 1987
Sixth impression 1993

Printed in Great Britain for
Hodder and Stoughton Educational,
a division of Hodder and Stoughton Limited,
Mill Road, Dunton Green, Sevenoaks, Kent
by St Edmundsbury Press Limited,
Bury St Edmunds, Suffolk
Photoset by Rowland Phototypesetting Limited,
Bury St Edmunds, Suffolk

Contents

Reading, Talking, Writing

WEATHER

Reading, Talking, Writing

DREAMS AND HAUNTINGS

Reading, Talking, Writing

PEOPLE

Reading, Talking, Writing

TOWN AND COUNTRY

Reading, Talking, Writing

To the Teacher

Since the first *Touchstones* series was launched there have been major changes in teaching methods and many exciting new poets writing for children have emerged. We have revised the series so that the basic concept of the 'teaching anthology' remains. This is still the most effective way of combining three key features: an up-to-date selection of poems; teaching approaches which are primarily concerned with the individual's responses; and activities —often in pairs or small groups—which will bring the poems off the page. While many of the poems in the original volumes are retained, we have been able to include a generous selection of verse from current writers. The teaching sections on 'Exploring Poems' and the activities suggested at the end of each group of poems in the 'Anthology' have been completely revised and expanded. Even so, books can only do so much; poetry lessons, in particular, depend for their success upon a sympathetic relationship between teacher and pupils. When this exists children can learn more about what language is and what language does from experiencing poetry than from any other form of language use. What is more, approached creatively—with ample opportunities for performance and individual involvement—poetry lessons can be fun for both teacher and pupils.

The pattern of our 'teaching anthology' is as follows. First, in 'Exploring Poems' (Part A), we introduce three main topics which give information about a particular aspect of poetry, illustrate by examples and engage the children in talking, reading, and writing about poems. The individual teacher is the best judge of just how and when to use this area of the book. Secondly, in the 'Anthology' (Part B), we have grouped the material so that the teacher will be able to deal with several poems, linked by some common quality of technique, subject matter, style or attitude, in any one lesson or sequence of lessons. Thirdly, at the end of each section in the 'Anthology' we have provided suggestions for encouraging the pupils to respond to the poems in a variety of ways: live performances, tape-recordings, personal writing, displays and so on. We consider that pupils should be offered the chance to experiment, to play with the words, sounds and shapes of poems in the same way that they play with paints and materials in an art lesson. Unless it is developed, such freedom can become mere licence. Teachers, therefore, will often want to help children redraft their first ideas. Ideally, the 'play' element leads to a delight in the discipline of form.

Opportunities for this kind of personal involvement offer children both a means of understanding and ways of developing a 'feel' for poems which are not only enjoyable in themselves but also provide the best foundation for a fuller appreciation of poetry in later years.

Finally, we hope it is evident from the approaches we adopt that we do not wish the books to be followed slavishly as a 'course'. Indeed, the distinction between material suited, for example, to a second as opposed to a first form must sometimes be arbitrary. Although the books are numbered from one to five and the topics and poems have been chosen to suit particular age groups, teachers will find sufficient flexibility in the arrangement to be able to select and modify the material according to their own tastes and the abilities of their pupils. We also suggest the building up of resources to complement our selections. A mini-library of slim volumes of poetry chosen by author is essential in any school; and there are hundreds of practical ideas in the following books:

Michael Benton and Geoff Fox: *Teaching Literature 9–14*, OUP

Peter Benton : *Pupil, Teacher Poem*, Hodder & Stoughton

Sandy Brownjohn : *Does it Have to Rhyme?* Hodder & Stoughton
What Rhymes with Secret? Hodder & Stoughton

Ted Hughes : *Poetry in the Making*, Faber

Michael Rosen : *I See a Voice*, Hutchinson

Stephen Tunnicliffe : *Poetry Experience*, Methuen

PART A

Exploring Poems

Shapes

(i) Patterns on the page

One of the first things that tells us we are looking at a poem rather than any other kind of writing is its shape on the page.

Flick through the pages of this book. As you see, poems come in all shapes and sizes. There are neat, squared-off verses of four lines each; long, wavering lines where there seems to be no sort of pattern; tall thin poems and short, chunky ones; there are even poems that are arranged on the page in a design or perhaps as a picture.

The shape of these poems is not an accident: writers choose the line length, the pattern on the page, the overall shape of the poem that best suits their purpose. They may choose one of the old, traditional forms such as the four line verse which is often used for ballads and poems that tell a story. For example, the old ballad about Sir Patrick Spens begins:

> The king sits in Dunfermline town
>   Drinking the blood-red wine:
> 'O where will I get a good sailor,
>   To sail this ship of mine?'

Later in this book you will find that much of the story of *The Ancient Mariner* is told in a similar way:

> 'I fear thee, ancient Mariner!
> I fear thy skinny hand!
> And thou art long, and lank, and brown,
> As is the ribbed sea sand.'

The simple form of such poems on the page and their regular rhymes and rhythm invite us to settle back and listen to a good story. Here's the beginning of another one:

> Mary stood in the kitchen
>   Baking a loaf of bread.
> An angel flew through the window.
>   'We've a job for you,' he said.

3

There is a reason for the pattern the words make, the form that the poet chooses for these stories. There is often an equally good reason for choosing a much freer form as D. H. Lawrence does for his poem *Bat*. Again it is a story but he himself is at the centre of it. He tells about the unnerving experience of suddenly realising that the creatures he is watching flying in the gathering gloom beneath the arches of the Ponte Vecchio bridge in Italy are no longer the swallows of daytime that he so likes but the bats of evening that he loathes:

Like a glove, a black glove thrown up at the light
And falling back.

Never swallows!
Bats!
The swallows are gone.

At a wavering instant the swallows give way to bats
By the Ponte Vecchio . . .
Changing guard.

Why do the lines take this shape? Why is the one word *Bats!* given a line all to itself? Why the two blank lines?

When you look at the poem *Mountain Lion* on p. 27 which is also by D. H. Lawrence, can you see how he shapes it in a similar way? By arranging the words like this he is telling us something about how he wants the poem to be read. You can see him doing something similar in his poem on p. 133, *Storm In the Black Forest*.

This way of writing is called *free verse* but that doesn't mean that the writer chops up the lines into uneven lengths just for the sake of being different. Look at the way another poet, George Macbeth, wrote about touching his cat, Peter:

You can touch
his
feet, only
if
he is relaxed.
He
doesn't like it.

(from *Fourteen Ways of Touching the Peter*)

He could have written this: 'You can touch his feet, only if he is relaxed. He doesn't like it.' Why do you think he set it out on the page as he did? How is he suggesting we might read the lines?

The arrangement of the words on the page helps us to 'see' the sleepy cat and to feel its response to the light touch of fingers upon its four paws.

Wilfrid Noyce, a mountaineer, wrote this poem at 21,200 feet. How do the short lines and the shape of this poem help him to tell his story and to make us feel what he felt?

Breathless

(Written at 21,200 feet on May 23rd)

Heart aches,
Lungs pant
The dry air
Sorry, scant.
Legs lift
And why at all?
Loose drift,
Heavy fall.
Prod the snow
Its easiest way;
A flat step
Is holiday.
Look up,
The far stone
Is many miles
Far and alone
Grind the breath
Once more and on;
Don't look up
Till journey's done.
Must look up,
Glasses are dim.
Wrench of hand
Is breathless limb.
Pause one step,
Breath swings back;
Swallow once,
Dry throat is slack.
Then on
To the far stone;

Don't look up,
Count the steps done.
One step,
One heart-beat,
Stone no nearer
Dragging feet.
Heart aches,
Lungs pant
The dry air
Sorry, scant.

WILFRID NOYCE

Certain words you would normally use if you were writing this description as a composition or part of a story are missed out.

What sort of words are these? Why do you think the writer chooses to leave them out?

In pairs or small groups prepare a reading of the poem for the rest of the class to give the feeling of the exhausted climber as he forces himself on towards the summit.

(ii) Picture poems

Sometimes writers arrange their poems so that the words actually make an outline picture or a recognisable shape on the page, which helps us to see and experience more clearly what is being described. In some cases, even if you hold the book so far away from you that you cannot read the words, you will have some idea of what the poems are about. The shape tells you.

Shape poems may be quite serious, but often writers enjoy playing with words and hope that you will too. Perhaps you already know *The Mouse's Tail* from Lewis Carroll's *Alice's Adventures in Wonderland*:

'Mine is a long and a sad tale,' said the Mouse, turning to Alice, and sighing.

'It *is* a long tail, certainly,' said Alice, looking down with wonder at the Mouse's tail; 'but why do you call it sad?' And she kept on puzzling about it while the Mouse was speaking so that her idea of the tale was something like this:

                    'Fury said to
               a mouse, That
               he met in the
                    house, "Let
                    us both go
                    to law: *I*
                    will prose-
                    cute *you.*—
                    Come, I'll
                    take no de-
                    nial: We
               must have
               the trial;
          For really
        this morn-
        ing I've
        nothing
        to do."
         Said the
          mouse to
          the cur.
           "Such a
             trial. dear
              sir. With
                no jury
                  or judge.
                  would
                  be wast-
                  ing our
                breath."
              "I'll he
            judge.
          I'll be
        jury."
          said
        cun-
        ning
        o l d
        Fury:
          "I'll
            t r y
             t h e
              whole
               cause.
                 and
                con-
                demn
              you to
        death".'

Of course this sort of thing upsets the printer, but, when you think
about it, there is no reason why poems, particularly those in free
verse, should not be more adventurous in shape. The French poet
Guillaume Apollinaire wrote a number of short picture-poems
called 'calligrams' in which he tried, by the shape of the verse, to
illustrate the thing being described. This is part of one which was
written when he was serving as an artilleryman with a battery of
heavy field guns in the First World War. What do the two shapes
represent?

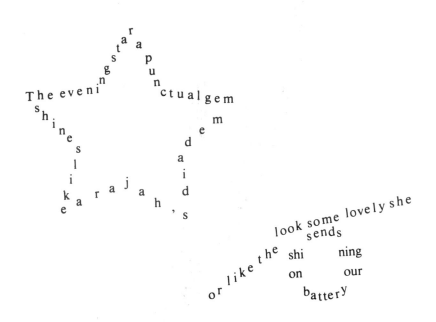

The evening star punctual gem shines like a raja's maid and sends look some lovely she or like the shining on our battery

A boy wrote about the first time his pet cat saw snow like this:

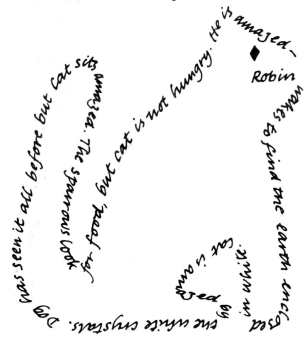

He is amazed –
Robin

Here is another shape poem like *Amazed Cat* only this time the words *fill* the shape instead of outlining it. Again it is by somebody of about your own age.

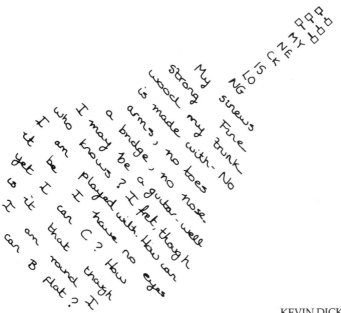

KEVIN DICKSON

And here is one that is really tricky to read but it does catch something of the jumpy, unpredictable nature of its subject:

r-p-o-p-h-e-s-s-a-g-r

                          r p-o-p-h-e-s-s-a-g-r
              who
a)s w(e loo)k
upnowgath
            PPEGORHRASS
                                    eringint(o-
aThe):l
        eA
            !p:
S

                                        a
                  (r
rivinG   .gRrEaPsPhOs)
                              to
rea(be)rran(com)gi(e)ngly
,grasshopper;

                        e. e. cummings

9

You can even shape a poem around the positions of a football team if you like! This one by Roger McGough takes some careful reading to sort out at first but it does make sense:

Cup-Final

T. O'Day

W. E. March   T. O. G. Lory

J. Usty   O. Uwait   N. See

G. O'Dow
A. Day   W. Ewill   N. Infa   H. I. Story

Young   N. Fast   M. O'Reskill   I. T. Sreally
W. Egot

A. L. L. Sewnup   W. E. Rethel   A. D. S. Whollrun

A. Round   W. Embley

W. I. Thecup

ROGER MCGOUGH

Now try writing a poem of your own designed to fit a shape. Start with something simple—a triangle, diamond or circle perhaps and then tackle something a bit more complicated. What words would you like to fit to the shape of a rocket, a church, an eye, a parachute, a snail, a fish, a snake . . .? Don't forget that the words and the shape should help each other.

If you need more ideas or examples, look at the Shapes section which begins on p. 27.

R. Bennet's poem *Wordcage* sums up what we have said in this section:

A
poet
crafts a cage with words,
and shapes it on the page
Holding
the fleeting thoughts
like
birds
within a fine wordcage.

Sound, Movement and Rhythm

(i) Sounds

. . . SLITHY . . . MIMSY . . . UFFISH . . .

What do you think the word 'slithy' could mean? What on earth are 'mimsy' and 'uffish'? Say them over to yourself a few times. Now quickly jot down what you think they might mean, any ideas they may suggest, or anything they might describe. It's no use looking in your dictionary: you won't find them there.

You may have heard the words before. They come from a non-sense poem by Lewis Carroll. As you read it or hear it read, listen to the strange sounds and see the pictures they conjure up in your mind's eye:

Jabberwocky

'Twas brillig, and the slithy toves
   Did gyre and gimble in the wabe:
All mimsy were the borogoves,
   And the mome raths outgrabe.

'Beware the Jabberwock, my son!
   The jaws that bite, the claws that catch!
Beware the Jubjub bird, and shun
   The frumious Bandersnatch!'

He took his vorpal sword in hand:
   Long time the manxome foe he sought—
So rested he by the Tumtum tree,
   And stood awhile in thought.

And as in uffish thought he stood,
   The Jabberwock, with eyes of flame,
Came whiffling through the tulgey wood,
   And burbled as it came!

One, two! One, two! And through and through
   The vorpal blade went snicker-snack!
He left it dead, and with its head
   He went galumphing back.

'And hast thou slain the Jabberwock?
   Come to my arms, my beamish boy!
O frabjous day! Callooh! Callay!'
   He chortled in his joy.

'Twas brillig, and the slithy toves
   Did gyre and gimble in the wave;
All mimsy were the borogoves,
   And the mome raths outgrabe.

LEWIS CARROLL

Lots of the words in the poem are pure invention. Lewis Carroll enjoyed making up 'uffish', 'tulgey', 'brillig', 'frabjous' and all the rest of his creations. They are what they suggest to us through their sound and the way they are used. They may be 'nonsense' but we cannot help ourselves from making a kind of sense of them as they trigger ideas and associations in our minds.

In Chapter Six of *Through the Looking Glass*, which is where the poem first appeared, Humpty Dumpty explains to Alice the meaning of some of the words. ' "*Brillig*" ', he says, 'means four o'clock in the afternoon—the time when you begin *broiling* things for dinner,' and ' "*slithy*" ' means "lithe and slimy" . . . there are two meanings packed up into one word.' Of course his explanations are not the only possible ones. Did 'brillig' and 'slithy' suggest something different to you?

So far you have tried to explain three of the words; now, on your own, jot down the ideas suggested to you by some of the others:

toves	gyre and gimble
mome raths	borogoves
frumious	outgrabe
manxome	vorpal
galumphing	beamish

Working in pairs or small groups, discuss and compare your ideas. How far do you agree?

Amazingly this nonsense poem has been translated into other languages. Here is the first verse in nonsense French and German:

Il brilgue: les toves lubricilleux
Se gyrent en vrillant dans le guave.
Enmimés sont les gougebosqueux
Et le momerade horsgrave.

(French)

Es brillig war. Die schlichten Toven
Wirrten und wimmelten in Waben;
Und aller-mumsige Burggoven
Die mohmen Rath' ausgraben.

(German)

Jabberwocky nonsense, it seems, is international. It is a poem that demands to be read aloud and to be enjoyed for its sound. In groups or as a whole class you could present a prepared dramatic reading of the poem with individual voices, chorus and sound effects to match. It could make a weird and wonderful tape-recording.

Why not experiment with words yourself? Try to write a nonsense poem of your own. Be careful not to use nonsense words too freely; Lewis Carroll uses quite a lot of everyday words as well as those of his own invention. One idea, if you can't think of how to get started, is to write a sequel to *Jabberwocky*. Look at the second verse again: the Jabberwock is only one of the three possible attackers the young man has to face. Write your own poem about either the Jubjub bird or the Bandersnatch.

Do you sometimes do the washing-up at home? If so, you will know the sound of the squelchy detergent bottle, the feel of wet rubber gloves, the joys of sloshing about with the porridge pan . . .

> Scouring out the porridge pot,
>   Round and round and round!
>
> Out with all the scraith and scoopery,
> Lift the eely ooly droopery,
> Chase the glubbery slubbery
>   gloopery
>   Round and round and round!

(from Sink Song, J. A. LINDON)

There are several invented words here but if you have ever washed up a porridge pan you will know how well they describe the rubbery skin and the slimy strings of porridge sticking to its sides and the sucking, slopping sounds of the 'glubbery slubbery gloopery'.

Here the writer chooses words to sound like the thing he is describing. There is a special word for this effect—it is called *onomatopoeia*. It's a long word for something very ordinary: we all of us use onomatopoeia when we use words like 'cuckoo', 'babble', 'boom', 'slurp', 'squelch' . . . Can you think of any more words whose sound suggests their meaning? Make a list: there are dozens.

Here are two more invented words which you will not find in a dictionary—'malooma' and 'taketi'. Jot down which name you think best describes each of these shapes. Can you say why?

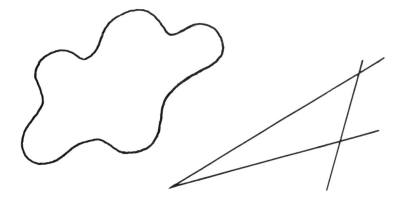

Your answers to these questions may suggest something about the way you think about the sounds of words and the kinds of associations they have for you. Here are a dozen words: working on your own or in pairs sort them out into two lists of six—one list for 'maloomas', the other for 'taketis'.

balloon	icicle	snatch	vicious
mushroom	oozing	picnic	lash
tripping	summer	puddle	volume

Compare your lists with those of others.
How did you decide which words to put in each list?
Did you find some words more difficult to classify than others?
Why do you think this was?

Your two lists of words are useful to show you how some words may suggest different qualities by their sounds and their associations: these may not only be 'malooma' qualities of roundness or bulkiness or 'taketi' qualities of sharpness and quickness, but also such things as warmth or coldness, lightness or heaviness.

Let's move from the sound of single words to the sound of whole lines. Again, either by yourself or in pairs, do the same kind of list-making for the following lines:

1. an icicle:
Feel the chilling spear
Sending shivers through my hand.
Cold and glacial knife.

2. a summer evening:
The velvet hum of evening

3. blades of grass:
Only some spires of bright green grass,
Transparently in sunshine quivering.

4. bodies falling lifeless:
With heavy thump, a lifeless lump,
They dropped down one by one.

5. the sound of bees:
And murmuring of innumerable bees

6. fishermen gutting fish at the docks:
                                  . . . the clockwork men

Incise and scoop the oily pouches, flip
The soft guts overboard . . .

                        . . . the slapping silver turns
To polished icy marble upon the deck.

Do you agree or disagree which list each should be in?
Did any seem to be a mixture?

(ii) Sound and movement

It is not just word sound and associations of course, it's also the way
that the lines *move* on the page that helps create pictures in our
mind's eye and works on our feelings. The movement of the
'clockwork' fishermen in the last example above can be heard as we
read the lines. Here's another description by the same writer: *listen*
to his description of pigeons cooing to themselves:

Only the warm dark dimples of sound
Slide like slow bubbles
From the contented throats.

Here, too, the noise is created by the repetition of certain letters and
the weighty sound of the heavy field guns in the first line is replaced
by the sharp, quick sounds of the rifle fire. Which letters produce
this effect? The technique of repeating certain letters has a special
name: *alliteration*.

Now read the following lines and discuss with a partner or in
groups how the sound and movement of the lines fit their subject:

1. a snake drinking from a water-trough:
He drank enough
And lifted his head, dreamily, as one who has drunken,
And flickered his tongue like a forked night on the air, so black,
Seeming to lick his lips . . .

2. children skating on a lake and shouting to each other:
So through the darkness and the cold we flew,
And not a voice was idle: with the din
Smitten, the precipices rang aloud;
The leafless trees and every icy crag
Tinkled like iron.

3. an old wolf:
Lopes on purpose, paddling the snow
Of the soft-blown winterlocked landscape,
Under the loaded branches in the hush of forests.

Whole lines can move quickly and sharply echoing the sound and movement of the thing being described as in the description of the rifle fire and the bat. They can move slowly and softly too as the wolf does in the forest or there can even be a blend of laziness and quickness as in the description of the snake.

Lines can move restlessly and irregularly too. *Listen* to this description of church bells ringing:

> The five old bells
> Are hurrying and stridently calling,
> Insisting, protesting
> They are right, yet clamorously falling
> Into gabbling confusion, without resting
> Like spattering shouts of an orator endlessly dropping
> From the tower on the town, but endlessly, never stopping.

How do the sound and movement help us to imagine the bells pealing out? What sounds are often repeated?

Here's another poem where sound and movement are all-important. Read it aloud and enjoy this dog's-eye view of a cat chase that should leave you breathless. There are several ways you could read this but you might find it helpful to have a group of two or three to speak the longer lines in chorus and to use single voices for the dog and cat noises:

Cat!

Cat!
Scat!
atter her, atter her,
Sleeky flatterer,
Spitfire chatterer,
Scatter her, scatter her
   Off her mat!
   Wuff!
   Wuff!
   Treat her rough!
Git her, git her,
Whiskery spitter!
Catch her, catch her,
Green-eyed scratcher!
   Slathery
   Slithery
   Hisser,
   Don't miss her!
Run till you're dithery,
   Hithery
   Thithery!
   Pfitts! pfitts!
   How she spits!
   Spitch! spatch!
   Can't she scratch!
Scritching the bark
Of the sycamore-tree,
She's reached her ark
And's hissing at me
   Pfitts! pfitts!
   Wuff! wuff!
   Scat,
   Cat!
   That's
   That!

ELEANOR·FARJEON

Recovered? If you can face another plunge into wild and whirling words try reading aloud this description of the great waterfall at Lodore. Split the lines between several different people perhaps

18

reading it as a 'round' with one voice starting the poem followed by another a second or two later so that the readings overlap:

from **The Cataract of Lodore**

The Cataract strong
Then plunges along,
Striking and raging
As if a war waging
Its caverns and rocks among:
Rising and leaping,
Sinking and creeping,
Swelling and sweeping,
Showering and springing,
Flying and flinging,
Writhing and ringing,
Eddying and whisking,
Spouting and frisking,
Turning and twisting,
Around and around
With endless rebound!
Smiting and fighting,
A sight to delight in;
Confounding, astounding,
Dizzying and deafening the ear with its sound,
Dividing and gliding and sliding,
And falling and brawling and sprawling,
And driving and riving and striving,
And sprinkling and twinkling and wrinkling,
And sounding and bounding and rounding,
And bubbling and troubling and doubling,
And grumbling and rumbling and tumbling,
And clattering and battering and shattering;
Retreating and beating and meeting and sheeting,
Delaying and straying and playing and spraying,
Advancing and prancing and glancing and dancing,
Recoiling, turmoiling and toiling and boiling,
And gleaming and streaming and steaming and beaming,
And rushing and flushing and brushing and gushing,
And flapping and rapping and clapping and slapping,
And curling and whirling and purling and twirling,

And thumping and plumping and bumping and jumping,
And dashing and flashing and splashing and clashing;
And so never ending, but always descending,
Sounds and motions for ever and ever are blending,
All at once and all o'er, with a mighty uproar,
And this way the Water comes down at Lodore.

ROBERT SOUTHEY

Pleased with it? Why not put your performance on to tape?

(iii) Sound, movement and rhythm

People like rhythm: it is part of them from before they are born. There are the minute personal rhythms of the heartbeat, pulse and breathing; the natural rhythms of our daily routine—sleeping, eating, washing, playing—which become part of the larger rhythms of time such as day following day and weeks turning into months and years. There is the rhythm of the day as light follows darkness only to be plunged into darkness again; the rhythm of the year as winter gives way to spring and summer to autumn and, for all living things there are the rhythms of birth, life and death. Very often, people spend much of their lives working at tasks involving repetitive movements and they sometimes develop rhythmic songs to help them in their work. The old sea shanties were examples of such work songs. Young children also like rhythmic songs ranging from nursery rhymes to the chants they make up when they are playing. Do you remember skipping rhymes, dipping rhymes, game rhymes from junior school? Tony Connor's poem on p. 58 may remind you of some of these. Can you think of any more examples of work or play songs?

As in music, rhythm in poetry is a kind of pattern which underlies and holds together the whole structure. Sometimes, as in music, the rhythm may be so strong that it is the most important part of the poem; sometimes it is deliberately played down and is quiet and unnoticed—but it is almost always there.

Another poem that is quite different in its sound and movement but that can be read using several voices in a similar way, is this one by John Agard. Keeping time can be tricky: you will probably find that the rhythm of the poem makes you break up words into two syllables echoing the insistent 'tap/tap' of the bird's beak so that 'carving' becomes 'car/ving'.

Woodpecker

Carving
tap/tap
music
out of
tap/tap
tree trunk
keep me
busy
whole day
tap/tap
long

tap/tap
pecker
birdsong
tap/tap
pecker
birdsong

tree bark
is tap/tap
drumskin
fo me beak
I keep
tap/tap
rhythm
fo forest
heartbeat

tap/tap
chisel beak
long
tap/tap
honey leak
song
pecker/tap
tapper/peck
pecker
birdsong

JOHN AGARD

Ted Hughes uses a quite different rhythm when he writes about the same subject and, although the rhythm is important, he makes his poem work for us much more through rhyme:

Woodpecker

Woodpecker is rubber-necked
   But has a nose of steel.
He bangs his head against the wall
   And cannot even feel.

When Woodpecker's jack-hammer head
   Starts up its dreadful din
Knocking the dead bough double dead
   How do his eyes stay in?

Pity the poor dead oak that cries
   In terrors and in pains.
But pity more Woodpecker's eyes
   And bouncing rubber brains.

TED HUGHES

We enjoy rhythms of all kinds. Sometimes, almost without realising it, we tap our feet, click our fingers in time to tunes, because the rhythm makes us want to *move* rhythmically, to be a part of the music ourselves. If you enjoy dancing, you will know the feeling of being completely taken over by the music almost as if you have escaped into another world. The player on drums or bass who provides the basic beat of the music usually holds the whole piece together.

In a limbo dance the dancer sways backwards closer and closer to the ground and almost parallel to it so as to pass under a very low bar. The dance dates back to the days of slavery when the only way that the wretched chained slaves could exercise in the dark, stinking holds of the old slave ships was by moving in this cramped fashion. Hear how the rhythm of limbo runs through every line of this poem. Once you have got the feel of the haunting limbo rhythm you will find it a good piece to dramatise as a group calling up different voices in turn:

Limbo

And limbo stick is the silence in front of me
limbo

limbo
limbo like me
limbo
limbo like me

long dark night is the silence in front of me
limbo
limbo like me

stick hit sound
and the ship like it ready

stick hit sound
and the dark still steady

limbo
limbo like me

long dark deck and the water surrounding me
long dark deck and the silence is over me

limbo
limbo like me

stick is the whip
and the dark deck is slavery

stick is the whip
and the dark deck is slavery

limbo
limbo like me

drum stick knock
and the darkness is over me

knees spread wide
and the water is hiding me

limbo
limbo like me

knees spread wide
and the dark ground is under me

down
down
down

and the drummer is calling me
limbo
limbo like me

sun coming up
and the drummers are praising me

out of the dark
and the dumb gods are raising me

up
up
up

and the music is saving me

hot
slow
step

on the burning ground.

EDWARD KAMAU BRATHWAITE

Movement, rhythm, sound and rhyme work *together*. We can't really talk about any one of these things by itself without thinking about the others. We think that Marjorie Boulton had the right idea when she wrote that you can't take an egg out of a cake that has been baked!

PART B

Anthology

Shapes

Mountain Lion

Climbing through the January snow, into the Lobo canyon
Dark grow the spruce-trees, blue is the balsam, water sounds
   still unfrozen, and the trail is still evident.

Men!
Two men!
Men! The only animal in the world to fear!

They hesitate.
We hesitate.
They have a gun.
We have no gun.

Then we all advance, to meet.

Two Mexicans, strangers, emerging out of the dark and
   snow and inwardness of the Lobo valley.
What are you doing here on this vanishing trail?

What is he carrying?
Something yellow.
A deer?

Que tiene, amigo?
Leon—*

*What have you got, friend?
A lion—

He smiles, foolishly, as if he were caught doing wrong
And we smile, foolishly, as if we didn't know.
He is quite gentle and dark-faced.

It is a mountain lion,
A long, long slim cat, yellow like a lioness.
Dead.
He trapped her this morning, he says, smiling foolishly.

Lift up her face,
Her round, bright face, bright as frost.
Her round, fine-fashioned head, with two dead ears;
And stripes in the brilliant frost of her face, sharp, fine dark
    rays,
Dark, keen, fine eyes in the brilliant frost of her face.
Beautiful dead eyes.

*Hermoso es!**   **It's beautiful*

They go out towards the open;
We go on into the gloom of Lobo.
And above the trees I found her lair,
A hole in the blood-orange brilliant rocks that stick up, a little
    cave,
And bones, and twigs, and a perilous ascent.

So, she will never leap up that way again, with the yellow
　　flash of a mountain lion's long shoot!
And her bright striped frost-face will never watch any more,
　　out of the shadow of the cave in the blood-orange rock,
Above the trees of the Lobo dark valley-mouth!

Instead, I look out.
And out to the dim of the desert, like a dream, never real;
To the snow of the Sangre de Cristo mountains, the ice of the
　　mountains of Picoris,
And near across at the opposite steep of snow, green trees
　　motionless standing in snow, like a Christmas toy.

And I think in this empty world there was room for me and a
　　mountain lion.
And I think in the world beyond, how easily we might spare
　　a million or two of humans
And never miss them.
Yet what a gap in the world, the missing white frost-face of
　　that slim yellow mountain lion!

D. H. LAWRENCE

29

insu nli gh t

o
verand
o
vering

A

onc
eup
ona
tim

e ne wsp aper
e. e. cummings

one

t

hi

s

snowflake

(a
  li
    ght

in

g)

is upon a gra

v

es

t

one
e. e. cummings

To a Snowflake

What heart could have thought you?—
Past our devisal
(O filigree petal!)
Fashioned so purely,
Fragilely, surely,
From what Paradisal
Imagineless metal,
Too costly for cost?
Who hammered you, wrought you,
From argentine vapour?—
'God was my shaper.
Passing surmisal,
He hammered, He wrought me,
From curled silver vapour,
To lust of His mind:—
Thou couldst not have thought me!
So purely, so palely,
Tinily, surely,
Mightily, frailly,
Insculpted and embossed,
With His hammer of wind,
And His graver of frost.'

FRANCIS THOMPSON

in Just-spring

in Just—
spring   when the world is mud—
luscious the little
lame balloonman

whistles far   and   wee

and eddieandbill come
running from marbles and
piracies and it's
spring

when the world is puddle-wonderful

the queer
old balloonman whistles
far   and   wee
and bettyandisabel come dancing

from hop-scotch and jump-rope and

it's
spring
and
    the

        goat-footed

balloonMan   whistles
far
and
wee

                    e. e. cummings

From **The Gecko**

(For J. P.)

I don't know how many thousand years
Of evolution have not taught the gecko
You can't jump *up* downwards.

Blue-flecked, pink-flecked, semi-transparent,
Sucker-footed, he creeps
Across the ceiling. He sees
With his extraordinary protuberant eyes
A fly, just hovering below him . . . He
                                    jumps
                                            and

Flick!
    He falls to the floor:
Poor little half-dazed lizard!

JOHN HEATH-STUBBS

Johnny Nolan

Johnny Nolan has a patch on his ass

Kids chase him
                  thru screendoor summers
Thru the back streets
                  of all my memories
Somewhere a man laments
                      upon a violin
A doorstep baby cries
                 and cries again
            like
            a
             ball
                bounced
                    down steps
Which helps the afternoon arise again
To a moment of remembered hysteria

Johnny Nolan has a patch on his ass

Kids chase him

                    LAWRENCE FERLINGHETTI

Spacepoem 3: Off Course

the golden flood   the weightless seat
the cabin song   the pitch black
the growing beard   the floating crumb
the shining rendezvous   the orbit wisecrack
the hot spacesuit   the smuggled mouth-organ
the imaginary somersault   the visionary sunrise
the turning continents   the space debris
the golden lifeline   the space walk
the crawling deltas   the camera moon
the pitch velvet   the rough sleep
the crackling headphone   the space silence
the turning earth   the lifeline continents
the cabin sunrise   the hot flood
the shining spacesuit   the growing moon
   the crackling somersault   the smuggled orbit
   the rough moon   the visionary rendezvous
   the weightless headphone   the cabin debris
   the floating lifeline   the pitch sleep
   the crawling camera   the turning silence
   the space crumb   the crackling beard
   the orbit mouth-organ   the floating song

EDWIN MORGAN

The Computer's First Christmas Card

jollymerry
hollyberry
jollyberry
merryholly
happyjolly
jollyjelly
jellybelly
bellymerry
hollyheppy
jollyMolly
marryJerry
merryHarry
hoppyBarry
heppyJarry
boppyheppy
berryjorry
jorryjolly
moppyjelly
Mollymerry
Jerryjolly
bellyboppy
jorryhoppy
hollymoppy
Barrymerry
Jarryhappy
happyboppy
boppyjolly
jollymerry
merrymerry
merrymerry
merryChris
ammerryasa
Chrismerry
asMERRYCHR
YSANTHEMUM

EDWIN MORGAN

36

Cats

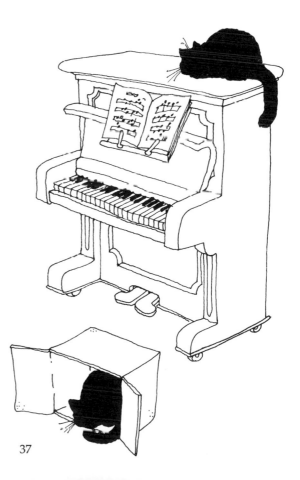

Cats sleep
Anywhere,
Any table,
Any chair,
Top of piano,
Window-ledge,
In the middle,
On the edge,
Open drawer,
Empty shoe,
Anybody's
Lap will do,
Fitted in a
Cardboard box,
In the cupboard
With your frocks—
Anywhere!
They don't care!
Cats sleep
Anywhere.

ELEANOR FARJEON

★ Writing. The poems in this section, like those on pp. 5–10, were all chosen because there is something unusual about the shape they make on the page.

—Choose a simple outline shape such as a cup, a tree, a bridge, an apple . . . Concentrate on the ideas it suggests . . . What is it *like*? . . . What does it remind you of? . . . What ideas or feelings come to mind? Jot them down. Now shape your words to follow the outline or to fill it completely.

—In *Breathless* on p. 5 Wilfrid Noyce uses the shape of the poem both to emphasise the strain felt by the climber and also to convey the idea of a high mountain. Try to write your own poem based on the idea of descent rather than ascent. You may, for example, imagine yourself as a deep-sea diver being lowered into the depths of the ocean; as a pot-holer worming his way deeper into the earth; or (rather more rapid these), as a swimmer diving or jumping from a high board, or a passenger in a descending lift. Whichever subject you choose you may find it useful to shape your poem in a similar way to *Breathless*.

—In e. e. cummings' poem on p. 30 notice how the words are arranged on the page to suggest the lazy, indirect fall of a snow-flake. You may be able to think of other things—falling leaves, a feather drifting to the ground, a sky-rocket on November 5th, soaring and bursting as it falls—which you could write about in a similar way.

—*The Computer's First Christmas Card* on p. 36 may suggest to you other ideas for poems written by computer. What might the same computer send as a *Baby's First Birthday Card*? How do you imagine the computer might greet someone or say goodbye? Try to get your computer poem down on paper. When you are satisfied with your ideas you might be able to key them in to a computer at home or school and see your poem as a real computer print-out.

★ Performing. Try reading *The Computer's First Christmas Card* and your own computer poems aloud using two or three voices and make a tape-recording of your performance.

—*Space Poem 3* (p. 35) is another poem that is good to perform and tape record. Use different people's voices for the different phrases. Decide on the tone of voice that you think best suits the poem.

—Eleanor Farjeon's *Cats* can be read by several different people each taking a line. Again it is worth aiming for a performance that you can tape record.

Sound, Movement and Rhythm

Thunder and Lightning

Blood punches through every vein
As lightning strips the windowpane.

Under its flashing whip, a white
Village leaps to light.

On tubs of thunder, fists of rain
Slog it out of sight again.

Blood punches the heart with fright
As rain belts the village night.

JAMES KIRKUP

Echo

'Who called?' I said, and the words
   Through the whispering glades,
Hither, thither, baffled the birds—
   'Who called? Who called?'

The leafy boughs on high
   Hissed in the sun;
The dark air carried my cry
   Faintingly on:

Eyes in the green, in the shade,
   In the motionless brake,
Voices that said what I said,
   For mockery's sake:

'Who cares?' I bawled through my tears;
   The wind fell low:
In the silence, 'Who cares? Who cares?'
   Wailed to and fro.

WALTER DE LA MARE

The Splendour Falls

The splendour falls on castle walls
    And snowy summits old in story:
The long light shakes across the lakes,
    And the wild cataract leaps in glory.
Blow, bugle, blow, set the wild echoes flying,
Blow, bugle; answer, echoes, dying, dying, dying.

O hark, O hear! how thin and clear,
    And thinner, clearer, farther going!
O sweet and far from cliff and scar
    The horns of Elfland faintly blowing!
Blow, let us hear the purple glens replying:
Blow, bugle; answer, echoes, dying, dying, dying.

O love, they die in yon rich sky,
    They faint on hill or field or river:
Our echoes roll from soul to soul,
    And grow for ever and for ever.
Blow, bugle, blow, set the wild echoes flying,
And answer, echoes, answer, dying, dying, dying.

LORD TENNYSON

The Blacksmiths

Swart, swarthy smiths besmattered with smoke
Drive me to death with the din of their dints.
Such noise on nights heard no one never;
What knavish cry and clattering of knocks!
The snub-nosed changelings cry after 'Coal! Coal!'
And blow their bellows till all their brains burst:
'Huff, puff!' pants one; 'Haff, paff!' another.
They spit and sprawl and spin many yarns;
They grind teeth and gnash them, and groan together,
Hot with the heaving of their hard hammers.
Aprons they have of hide of the bull.
Their shanks are shielded from the fierce sparks:
Heavy hammers they have, that are hard handled;
Stark strokes they strike on an anvil of steel.
Lus, bus! Las, das! they strike in rotation:
The Devil destroy such a doleful din.
The master lengthens a little piece, belabours a
   smaller,
Twines the two together, and strikes a treble note
Tik, tak! Hic, hac! Tiket, taket! Tik, tak!
Lus, bus! Las, das! such lives they lead
All horseshoers; Christ give them sorrow
For none for these water burners at night may rest

ANON.

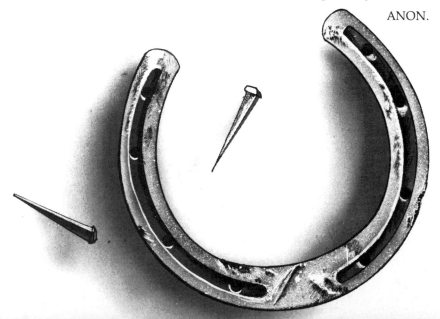

Pleasant Sounds

The rustling of leaves under the feet in woods and under
    hedges;
The crumping of cat-ice and snow down wood-rides, narrow
    lanes and every street causeway;
Rustling through a wood or rather rushing, while the wind
    halloos in the oak-top like thunder;
The rustle of birds' wings startled from their nests or flying
    unseen into the bushes;
The whizzing of larger birds overhead in a wood, such as
    crows, paddocks,* buzzards;   *kites
The trample of robins and woodlarks on the brown leaves,
    andthe patter of squirrels on the green moss;
The fall of an acorn on the ground, the pattering of nuts on
    the hazel branches as they fall from ripeness;
The flirt of ground-lark's wing from the stubbles—how
    sweet such pictures on dewy mornings, when the dew
    flashes from its brown feathers!

                                                    JOHN CLARE

In the Kitchen

In the Kitchen,
After the aimless
Chatter of the plates,
The murmurings of the gas,
The chuckle of the water pipes
And the sharp exchanges
Of knives, forks and spoons,
Comes the serious quiet,
When the sink slowly clears its throat
And you can hear the occasional rumble
Of the refrigerator's tummy
As it digests the cold.

JOHN COTTON

Half Asleep

Half asleep
And half awake
I drift like a boat
On an empty lake.
And the sounds in the house
And the street that I hear
Though far away sound very clear.
That's my sister Betty
Playing by the stairs
Shouting like teacher
At her teddy bears.
I can hear Mum chatting
To the woman next door
And the tumble drier
Vibrates through the floor.
That's Alan Simpson
Playing guitar
While his Dad keeps trying
To start their car.
Dave the mechanic
Who's out on strike
Keeps revving and tuning
His Yamaha bike.
From the open window
Across the street
On the August air
Drifts a reggae beat.
At four o'clock
With a whoop and a shout
The kids from St John's
Come tumbling out.
I can hear their voices
Hear what they say
And I play in my head
All the games that they play.

GARETH OWEN

45

Whisper Whisper

whisper whisper
whisper whisper
goes my sister
down the phone

whisper whisper
go the beech leaves
breathing in the
wind alone

whisper whisper
whisper whisper
slips the river
on the stone

whisper whisper
go my parents
when they whisper
on their own

I don't mind the
whisper whisper
whisper whisper
it's a tune

sometimes though
I wish the whisper
whisperings would
shut up soon

KIT WRIGHT

Snoozing by the Boozer

All day outside the boozer snores
The boozer-keeper's big brown dog
And carefully each boozer-user
Coming to or from the boozer
Steps around the shaggy snoozer,
    Dumped there like a log.

It chanced a fellow named de Souza
(An American composer)
Once was passing by the boozer
Humming to himself a Blues. A
Dog-enthuser, this de Souza,
So he halted by the boozer.
With his stick he poked the snoozer.
'Big brown dog,' he said, 'say who's a
    Good boy then?' This shows a

Lack of knowledge of the boozer-
Keeper's dog. It is a bruiser,
    Not a dreamy dozer.

Up it sprang and ate de Souza,
The American composer.
He is dead, the dog-enthuser.

Don't poke dogs outside the boozer.
You are bound to be the loser.

                                KIT WRIGHT

Cat

To plan plan to create to have
whiskers cool carat silver ready and curved
bristling

to plan plan to create to have
eyes green doors that dilate greenest
pouncers

to be ready rubber ball ready
feet bouncers cool fluid in
tension

to be steady steady claws all
attention to wait wait and create
pouncing

to be a cat eeling through alleys
slipping through windows of odours
to feel swiftness slowly

to halt at the gate hearing
unlocking whispers paper feet wrapping
potatoes and papers

to hear nicely mice spider feet
scratching great horny nails
catching a fire flies wire legs etch-

ing yet stretching beyond this arch
untriumphant lazily rubb-
ing the soft fur of home

EDWARD KAMAU BRATHWAITE

The Kangaroo's coff

*A Poem for Children Ill in Bed, Indicating to Them
the Oddities of our English Orthography**   *spelling*

The eminent Professor Hoff
Kept, as a pet, a Kangaroo
Who, one March day, started a coff
That very soon turned into floo.

Before the flu carried him off
To hospital (still with his coff),
A messenger came panting through
The door, and saw the Kangarough.

The Kangaroo lay wanly there
Within the Prof's best big armchere,
Taking (without the power to chew)
A sip of lemonade or tew.

'O Kangaroo,' the fellow said,
'I'm glad you're not already daid,
For I have here (pray do not scoff)
Some stuff for your infernal coff.

'If you will take these powdered fleas,
And just a tiny lemon squeas
Mixed with a little plain tapwater,
They'll cure you. Or at least they ater.'

Prof Hoff then fixed the medicine,
Putting the fleas and lemon ine
A glass of water, which he brought
The Kangaroo as he'd been tought.

The Kangaroo drank down the draught,
Shivered and scowled—then oddly laught
And vaulted out of the armchair
Before the Prof's astonished stair—

Out of the window, in the air
Up to the highest treetop whair
He sat upon the topmost bough
And chortled down, 'Look at me nough!'

The messenger would not receive
Reward for this, but answered, 'Weive
Done our best, and that's reward
Enough, my very learned lard'

(By which he meant Professor Hoff).
As for the Kangaroo, he blew
A kiss down as the man rode off,
A cured and happy Kangarew—

As you may be, when you have read
This tale I wrote lying in bead.

                              ANTHONY THWAITE

51

Hints on Pronunciation for Foreigners

I take it you already know
Of tough and bough and cough and dough?
Others may stumble but not you,
On hiccough, thorough, lough and through?
Well done! And now you wish, perhaps,
To learn of less familiar traps?

Beware of heard, a dreadful word
That looks like bears and sounds like bird,
And dead: it's said like bed, not bead—
For goodness sake don't call it 'deed'!
Watch out for meat and great and threat
(They rhyme with suite and straight and debt.)

A moth is not a moth in mother
Nor both in bother, broth in brother,
And here is not a match for there
Nor dear and fear for bear and pear,
And then there's dose and rose and lose—
Just look them up—and goose and choose,
And cork and work, and card and ward,
And font and front and word and sword,
And do and go and thwart and cart—
Come, come, I've hardly made a start!
A dreadful language? Man alive!
I'd mastered it when I was five!

ANON.

Inversnaid

This darksome burn, horseback brown,
His rollrock highroad roaring down,
In coop and in comb the fleece of his foam
Flutes and low to the lake falls home.

A wind-puff bonnet of fáwn-fróth
Turns and twindles over the broth
Of a pool so pitchblack, féll-frówning,
It rounds and rounds Despair to drowning.

Degged with dew, dappled with dew
Are the groins of the braes that the brook treads through,
Wiry heathpacks, flitches of fern,
And the beadbonny ash that sits over the burn.

What would the world be, once bereft
Of wet and of wildness? Let them be left,
O let them be left, wildness and wet;
Long live the weeds and the wilderness yet.

G. M. HOPKINS

The Quarry

O what is that sound which so thrills the ear
   Down in the valley drumming, drumming?
Only the scarlet soldiers, dear,
   The soldiers coming.

O what is that light I see flashing so clear
   Over the distance brightly, brightly?
Only the sun on their weapons, dear,
   As they step lightly.

O what are they doing with all that gear,
   What are they doing this morning, this morning?
Only their usual manoeuvres, dear,
   Or perhaps a warning.

O why have they left the road down there,
   Why are they suddenly wheeling, wheeling?
Perhaps a change in their orders, dear,
   Why are you kneeling?

O haven't they stopped for the doctor's care,
   Haven't they reined their horses, their horses?
Why they are none of them wounded, dear,
   None of these forces.

O is it the parson they want, with white hair,
   Is it the parson, is it, is it?
No, they are passing his gateway, dear,
   Without a visit.

O it must be the farmer who lives so near.
   It must be the farmer so cunning, so cunning?
They have passed the farmyard already, dear,
   And now they are running.

O where are you going? Stay with me here!
   Were the vows you swore deceiving, deceiving?
No, I promised to love you, dear,
   But I must be leaving.

O it's broken the lock and splintered the door,
   O it's the gate where they're turning, turning
Their boots are heavy on the floor
   And their eyes are burning.

                                    W. H. AUDEN

Tarantella

Do you remember an Inn,
Miranda?
Do you remember an Inn?

And the tedding and the spreading
Of the straw for a bedding,
And the fleas that tease in the High Pyrenees,
And the wine that tasted of the tar?
And the cheers and the jeers of the young muleteers
(Under the vine of the dark verandah)?
Do you remember an Inn, Miranda,
Do you remember an Inn?
And the cheers and the jeers of the young muleteers
Who hadn't got a penny,
And who weren't paying any,
And the hammer at the doors and the Din?
And the Hip! Hop! Hap!
Of the clap
Of the hands to the twirl and the swirl
Of the girl gone chancing,
Glancing,
Dancing,
Backing and advancing,
Snapping of a clapper to the spin
Out and in—
And the Ting, Tong, Tang of the Guitar!
Do you remember an inn,
Miranda?
Do you remember an Inn?
Never more;
Miranda,
Never more.
Only the high peaks hoar:
And Aragon a torrent at the door.
No sound
In the walls of the Halls where falls
The tread
Of the feet of the dead to the ground
No sound:
But the boom
Of the far Waterfall like Doom.

HILAIRE BELLOC

Skimbleshanks: The Railway Cat

There's a whisper down the line at 11.39
When the Night Mail's ready to depart,
Saying 'Skimble where is Skimble has he gone to hunt the
    thimble?
We must find him or the train can't start.'
All the guards and all the porters and the stationmaster's
    daughters
They are searching high and low,
Saying 'Skimble where is Skimble for unless he's very nimble
Then the Night Mail just can't go.'
At 11.42 when the signal's nearly due
And the passengers are frantic to a man—
Then Skimble will appear and he'll saunter to the rear:
He's been busy in the luggage van!
    He gives one flash of his glass-green eyes
        And the signal goes 'All Clear!'
    And we're off at last for the northern part
        Of the Northern Hemisphere!

You may say that by and large it is Skimble who's in charge
Of the Sleeping Car Express.
From the driver and the guards to the bagmen playing cards
He will supervise them all, more or less.
Down the corridor he paces and examines all the faces
Of the travellers in the First and in the Third;
He establishes control by a regular patrol
And he'd know at once if anything occurred.
He will watch you without winking and he sees what you are
    thinking
And it's certain that he doesn't approve
Of hilarity and riot, so the folk are very quiet
When Skimble is about and on the move.
    You can play no pranks with Skimbleshanks!
        He's a Cat that cannot be ignored;
    So nothing goes wrong on the Northern Mail
        When Skimbleshanks is aboard.

Oh it's very pleasant when you have found your little den
With your name written up on the door.
And the berth is very neat with a newly folded sheet
And there's not a speck of dust on the floor.
There is every sort of light—you can make it dark or bright;
There's a handle that you turn to make a breeze.
There's a funny little basin you're supposed to wash your
    face in
And a crank to shut the window if you sneeze.
Then the guard looks in politely and will ask you very
    brightly
'Do you like your morning tea weak or strong?'
But Skimble's just behind him and was ready to remind him,
For Skimble won't let anything go wrong.
    And when you creep into your cosy berth
        And pull up the counterpane,
    You ought to reflect that it's very nice
    To know that you won't be bothered by mice—
You can leave all that to the Railway Cat.
    The Cat of the Railway Train!

In the watches of the night he is always fresh and bright;
Every now and then he has a cup of tea
With perhaps a drop of Scotch while he's keeping on the
    watch,
Only stopping here and there to catch a flea.
You were fast asleep at Crewe and so you never knew
That he was walking up and down the station;
You were sleeping all the while he was busy at Carlisle,
Where he greets the stationmaster with elation.
But you saw him at Dumfries, where he speaks to the police
If there's anything they ought to know about:
When you get to Gallowgate there you do not have to wait—
For Skimbleshanks will help you to get out!
    He gives you a wave of his long brown tail
        Which says: 'I'll see you again!
    You'll meet without fail on the Midnight Mail
        The Cat of the Railway Train.'

T. S. ELIOT

Child's Bouncing Song

Molly Vickers
wets her knickers,
Georgie's father's big and black,
cream on Sunday
milk on Monday,
I'm the cock of all the back.

Tell me who's a
bigger boozer
Mister Baker beats them all,
from his lorry
watch him hurry,
touch the ground and touch the wall.

Who're the gentry
down our entry—
Mrs Smith's got two TV's.
What if her coat
is a fur coat,
all her kids are full of fleas.

Joan loves Harry,
Jack will marry
Edna when they both grow up,
I'll announce it,
bounce bounce bounce it,
our dog Whisker's had a pup.

High and low and
to and fro and
down the street and up the hill,
Mrs Cuthbert's
husband snuffed it,
she got nothing from his will.

Mister, mister,
Shirley's sister
won a prize on Blackpool prom,
mam'll smother
our kid brother
when the school inspectors come

Skip and hopping
I'm off shopping,
Tuesday night it's pie for tea,
please to take this
ball and make this
song of bouncing song for me.

TONY CONNOR

Limbo Dancer's Mantra*

LIMB/BOW

Pronounce dem
two syllable
real slow
you hear me
real slow

LIMB/BOW

Savour dem
two syllable
till glow
spread from head
to tip of toe

LIMB/BOW

Contemplate dem
two syllable
in vertigo
of drum tempo

LIMBO

Meditate on dem
two syllable
calm as zero
vibrate to sound
let mind go

and forget the stick
I tell you
don't think about the stick

that will take care of itself

JOHN AGARD

*A word that is said or
chanted as an incantation
or magic spell

★ **Writing.** Sounds like . . . What *do* things sound like? What does the roar of a football crowd sound like? The beating of your heart when you've been running? The tramp of marching soldiers' boots? The cry of a seagull?

—What are they *like*? Write down as many comparisons as you can for these examples and add your own. Choose the ones you like best and write your own poem called *Sounds Like*.

Sounds funny . . . Do you remember how Lewis Carroll invented 'nonsense' words for his poem *Jabberwocky* on p. 11?

—Now try to invent your own nonsense words to suggest the sound and feeling of the following:

the first helping of jelly being spooned from a large bowl;

fingernails or chalk scraping down a blackboard;

bathwater going down a plughole.

As before, add your own ideas and write your own poem called *Sounds Funny*.

Sounds good . . . Jot down quickly a list of sounds that you like. Perhaps the rustle of sweet papers, the sound of the bell at the end of school, your favourite group.

Sounds bad . . . Now do the same for sounds you hate . . . Perhaps the whine of the dentist's drill, the sound of the bell at the beginning of school, a terrible group.

When you have made your jottings try to write a poem contrasting your likes and dislikes. You could begin each line with either 'The sound I like is . . .' or 'The sound I hate is . . .' Or you could keep your two lists apart and write two poems, one called *Sounds Good*, the other called *Sounds Bad*.

Half Asleep, the poem on p. 45, describes the sounds somebody hears when daydreaming sleepily on a warm August afternoon. John Cotton's poem *In The Kitchen* describes the odd sounds heard in a kitchen when the house is quiet.

—Try to imagine yourself lying in bed in the morning when you can hear but do not see what is going on around you—the chink of milkbottles . . . the 'thunk' of the letterbox . . . voices and traffic outside . . . sounds from the kitchen . . . what else? Try to collect your ideas into a poem that describes this time of day.

★ **Performing.** Most of the poems in this section are ideal for reading aloud—some are riotous and loud, others much quieter and more thoughtful.

—Try reading Kit Wright's poem *Whisper, Whisper* using just two voices, one person reads the words 'whisper, whisper' each time they appear and the other reads the rest of the poem.

—Another poem that goes well with two voices is *Cat* by Edward Brathwaite (p. 48). Take a group of lines each in turn.

—*The Quarry* by W. H. Auden on p. 53 is written for two voices. See if you can communicate the gradual build up of tension in the poem from the uncertain tone of the first question to the horrified realisation of the last.

—*Child's Bouncing Song* by Tony Connor will probably remind you of playground games where you catch and bounce a ball to all sorts of complicated patterns and try to say a rhyme at the same time. Do you remember any of these? Try to perform Tony Connor's poem yourselves using a new voice for each verse. If you like you can add your own verses to the poem; start with a person's name and try to keep the rhythm the same.

—There ought to be a prize for anyone who can read the two poems on pp. 50 and 52 aloud without making a mistake. Try them and see.

—*Tarantella* (p. 54) by Hilaire Belloc is written to suggest the rhythm of a whirling Italian dance called the tarantella. (Believe it or not, it was supposed to cure people who had been bitten by the poisonous tarantula spider.) It is quite a tongue twister to read aloud and has a tricky rhythm. Have a go yourself.

—*Skimbleshanks: The Railway Cat* on p. 56 is written to suggest the rhythm of an old-fashioned steam railway engine. Divide the poem into sections to be read by groups or single voices and hear the different rhythms of the train as it pounds down the line, clatters over points and finally slows to a halt.

With all of these poems it is a good idea to give your performance to the rest of the class or to make a tape recording.

Creatures

Carrion

A yellowhammer in her mouth, the cat came mewing
To me. It was such a bird as I had seen
Skim the hedge like a ball of sun
Hurled by a starchild gaming in the wheat.

That was in summer. Now it is autumn,
I burning the leaves of a brave year dead
And gazing at the yellowhammer the cat abandoned,
Shrunken, soaked, but with a bright plume yet.

I stir the body: it is a shell stuffed with maggots.
They uncurl, startled by this threat to life—
And I, with human—so far holy!—love,
Hate maggots and cat, and long for golden wings.

CLIFFORD DYMENT

The Jaguar

The apes yawn and adore their fleas in the sun.
The parrots shriek as if they were on fire, or strut
Like cheap tarts to attract the stroller with the nut.
Fatigued with indolence, tiger and lion

Lie still as the sun. The boa-constrictor's coil
Is a fossil. Cage after cage seems empty, or
Stinks of sleepers from the breathing straw.
It might be painted on a nursery wall.

But who runs like the rest past these arrives
At a cage where the crowd stands, stares, mesmerised,
As a child at a dream, at a jaguar hurrying enraged
Through prison darkness after the drills of his eyes

On a short fierce fuse. Not in boredom—
The eye satisfied to be blind in fire,
By the bang of blood in the brain deaf the ear—
He spins from the bars, but there's no cage to him

More than to the visionary his cell:
His stride is wildernesses of freedom:
The world rolls under the long thrust of his heel.
Over the cage floor the horizons come.

TED HUGHES

The Tyger

Tyger! Tyger! burning bright
In the forests of the night,
What immortal hand or eye
Could frame thy fearful symmetry?

In what distant deeps or skies
Burnt the fire of thine eyes?
On what wings dare he aspire?
What the hand dare seize the fire?

And what shoulder, and what art,
Could twist the sinews of thy heart?
And when thy heart began to beat,
What dread hand? and what dread feet?

What the hammer? what the chain?
In what furnace was thy brain?
What the anvil? what dread grasp
Dare its deadly terrors clasp?

When the stars threw down their spears,
And water'd heaven with their tears,
Did he smile his work to see?
Did he who made the Lamb make thee?

Tyger! Tyger! burning bright
In the forests of the night,
What immortal hand or eye,
Dare frame thy fearful symmetry?

WILLIAM BLAKE

Pigeons

They paddle with staccato feet
In powder-pools of sunlight,
Small blue busybodies
Strutting like fat gentlemen
With hands clasped
Under their swallowtail coats;
And, as they stump about,
Their heads like tiny hammers
Tap at imaginary nails
In non-existent walls.
Elusive ghosts of sunshine
Slither down the green gloss
Of their necks an instant, and are gone.

Summer hangs drugged from sky to earth
In limpid fathoms of silence:
Only warm dark dimples of sound
Slide like slow bubbles
From the contented throats.

Raise a casual hand—
With one quick gust
They fountain into air.

RICHARD KELL

Hedgehog

Twitching the leaves just where the drainpipe clogs
In ivy leaves and mud, a purposeful
Creature at night about its business. Dogs
Fear his stiff seriousness. He chews away

At beetles, worms, slugs, frogs. Can kill a hen
With one snap of his jaws, can taunt a snake
To death on muscled spines. Old countrymen
Tell tales of hedgehogs sucking a cow dry.

But this one, cramped by houses, fences, walls,
Must have slept here all winter in that heap
Of compost, or have inched by intervals
Through tidy gardens to this ivy bed.

And here, dim-eyed, but ears so sensitive
A voice within the house can make him freeze,
He scuffs the edge of danger; yet can live
Happily in our nights and absences.

A country creature, wary, quiet and shrewd,
He takes the milk we give to him, when we're
   gone.
At night, our slamming voices must seem crude
To one who sits and waits for silences.

ANTHONY THWAITE

The Tom-cat

At midnight in the alley
  A Tom-cat comes to wail,
And he chants the hate of a million years
  As he swings his snaky tail.

Malevolent, bony, brindled,
  Tiger and devil and bard,
His eyes are coals from the middle of Hell
  And his heart is black and hard.

He twists and crouches and capers
  And bares his curved sharp claws,
And he sings to the stars of the jungle nights,
  Ere cities were, or laws.

Beast from a world primeval,
  He and his leaping clan,
When the blotched red moon leers over the roofs
  Give voice to their scorn of man.

He will lie on a rug to-morrow
  And lick his silky fur,
And veil the brute in his yellow eyes
  And play he's tame and purr.

But at midnight in the alley
  He will crouch again and wail,
And beat the time for his demon's song
  With the swing of his demon's tail.

DON MARQUIS

The Singing Cat

It was a little captive cat
    Upon a crowded train
His mistress takes him from his box
    To ease his fret and pain.

She holds him tight upon her knee
    The graceful animal
And all the people look at him
    He is so beautiful.

But oh he pricks and oh he prods
    And turns upon her knee
Then lifteth up his innocent voice
    In plaintive melody.

He lifteth up his innocent voice
    He lifteth up, he singeth
And to each human countenance
    A smile of grace he bringeth.

He lifteth up his innocent paw
    Upon her breast he clingeth
And everybody cries, Behold
    The cat, the cat that singeth.

He lifteth up his innocent voice
    He lifteth up, he singeth
And all the people warm themselves
    In the love his beauty bringeth.

STEVIE SMITH

Death of a Fly

Raising my pen to put a point
On the page, a dot over an i,
An unsteadily veering fly
Collides in a three-point landing, and settles.
Then, as if carving a joint,
It carefully sharpens its legs,
Sitting up the way a dog begs.
I notice a wing shed like a petal.
It has come here to die.
And my dot, streaked now with blood,
Turns the colour of mud.

ALAN ROSS

The Disclosure

From the shrivelling gray
silk of its cocoon
a creature slowly
   is pushing out
to stand clear—

            not a butterfly,
                petal that floats at will across
                the summer breeze

            not a furred
            moth of the night
                crusted with indecipherable
                gold—

some primal-shaped, plain-winged, day-flying thing.

DENISE LEVERTOV

Two Performing Elephants

He stands with his forefeet on the drum
and the other, the old one, the pallid hoary female
must creep her great bulk beneath the bridge of him.

On her knees, in utmost caution
all agog, and curling up her trunk
she edges through without upsetting him.
Triumph! the ancient, pig-tailed monster!

When her trick is to climb over him
with what shadow-like slow carefulness
she skims him, sensitive
as shadows from the ages gone and perished
in touching him, and planting her round feet.

While the wispy, modern children, half-afraid,
watch silent. The looming of the hoary, far-gone ages
is too much for them.

D. H. LAWRENCE

The Heron

The heron stands in water where the swamp
Has deepened to the blackness of a pool,
Or balances with one leg on a hump
Of marsh grass heaped above a musk-rat hole.

He walks the shallow with an antic grace.
The great feet break the ridges of the sand,
The long eye notes the minnow's hiding
    place.
His beak is quicker than a human hand.

He jerks a frog across his bony lip,
Then points his heavy bill above the wood.
The wide wings flap but once to lift him up.
A single ripple starts from where he stood.

THEODORE ROETHKE

The Heron

On lonely river-mud a heron alone
Of all things moving—water, reeds, and mist—
Maintains his sculptured attitude of stone.
A dead leaf floats on the sliding river, kissed
By its own reflection in a brief farewell.
Movement without sound; the evening drifts
On autumn tides of colour, light, and smell
Of warm decay; and now the heron lifts
Enormous wings in elegy; a grey
Shadow that seems to bear the light away.

PHOEBE HESKETH

The Rabbit

(*After Prévert*)

We are going to see the rabbit,
We are going to see the rabbit.
Which rabbit, people say?
Which rabbit, ask the children?
Which rabbit?
The only rabbit,
The only rabbit in England,
Sitting behind a barbed-wire fence
Under the floodlights, neon lights,
Sodium lights,
Nibbling grass
On the only patch of grass
In England, in England
(Except the grass by the hoardings
Which doesn't count.)
We are going to see the rabbit
And we must be there on time.

First we shall go by escalator,
Then we shall go by underground,
And then we shall go by motorway
And then by helicopterway,
And the last ten yards we shall have to go
On foot.

And now we are going
All the way to see the rabbit,
We are nearly there,
We are longing to see it,
And so is the crowd
Which is here in thousands

With mounted policemen
And big loudspeakers
And bands and banners,

And everyone has come a long way.
But soon we shall see it
Sitting and nibbling
The blades of grass
On the only patch of grass
In—but something has gone wrong!
Why is everyone so angry,
Why is everyone jostling
And slanging and complaining?

The rabbit has gone,
Yes, the rabbit has gone.
He has actually burrowed down into the earth
And made himself a warren, under the earth,
Despite all these people.
And what shall we do?
What *can* we do?

It is all a pity, you must be disappointed,
Go home and do something else for today,
Go home again, go home for today.
For you cannot hear the rabbit, under the earth,
Remarking rather sadly to himself, by himself,
As he rests in his warren, under the earth:
'It won't be long, they are bound to come,
They are bound to come and find me, even here.'

ALAN BROWNJOHN

The Song of the Whale

Heaving mountain in the sea,
Whale, I heard you
Grieving.

Great whale, crying for your life,
Crying for your kind, I knew
How we would use
Your dying:

Lipstick for our painted faces,
Polish for our shoes.

Tumbling mountain in the sea,
Whale, I heard you
Calling.

Bird-high notes, keening, soaring:
At their edge a tiny drum
Like a heartbeat.

We would make you
Dumb.

In the forest of the sea,
Whale, I heard you
Singing,

Singing to your kind.
We'll never let you be.
Instead of life we choose

Lipstick for our painted faces,
Polish for our shoes.

KIT WRIGHT

Meeting

As I went home on the old wood road,
    With my basket and lesson book,
A deer came out of the tall trees
    And down to drink at the brook.

Twilight was all about us,
    Twilight and tree on tree;
I looked straight into its great, strange eyes,
    And the deer looked back at me.

Beautiful, brown, and unafraid,
    Those eyes returned my stare;
And something with neither sound nor name
    Passed between us there.

Something I shall not forget—
    Something still, and shy, and wise—
In the dimness of the woods
    From a pair of gold-flecked eyes.

RACHEL FIELD

★ **Performing** — *The Song of The Whale* (p. 76) can be read by two or more voices with several people joining in to read the chorus lines which are printed in italics.

— *The Tyger* (p. 65) was written by William Blake nearly 200 years ago. After hearing it read, it is worth spending some time discussing the poem in a small group. When you think you have a feel for it try a group reading of the poem. You might choose to speak the first and last verses in chorus as a group and to give the other verses to four different voices.

— *The Tom-Cat* (p. 68) is another poem that can be divided up and read aloud by several different voices.

★ **Drama** —Alan Brownjohn's poem *The Rabbit* can simply be split up between different voices and read aloud, but really it cries out to be acted as well. There is a main voice—maybe two or three —almost like those of parents or teachers; there is the voice of the crowd and there are the voices of the children; there is the voice of a public announcement telling people to go home and, finally, there is the small, sad voice of the rabbit. And as the story unfolds there is the journey which all the people make by escalator, underground, motorway, helicopter and on foot to where the rabbit lives. You will probably need a fairly large space to work in like a hall or drama room.

★ **Looking and writing.** Richard Kell's poem *Pigeons* (p. 66) is full of details about how the pigeons move, what they look like, the sounds they make. All the time he is comparing the pigeons to other things—they strut 'like fat gentlemen', their heads are 'like tiny hammers' tapping 'imaginary nails'. These comparisons help us to see the picture more clearly in our mind's eye.

—Choose a creature you know well—something you can imagine clearly. It may be your pet cat or dog, a canary, goldfish, gerbil or hamster. Concentrate on its movement . . . what words best describe it? What is it *like*? Concentrate on its appearance . . . what words best describe it? What is it *like*? Concentrate on any sound it may make . . . what words best describe it? What is it *like*?

Jot down your ideas. Look back at what you have written. Try to shape your ideas into a poem that describes the creature you were imagining.

Ballads and Stories

I Started Early

I started early, took my dog,
   And visited the sea.
The mermaids in the basement
   Came out to look at me

And frigates in the upper floor
   Extended hempen hands,
Presuming me to be a mouse
   Aground upon the sands,

But no man moved me till the tide
   Went past my simple shoe
And past my apron and my belt
   And past my bodice too,

And made as he would eat me up
   As wholly as a dew
Upon a dandelion's sleeve;
   And then I started too

And he, he followed close behind;
   I felt his silver heel
Upon my ankle, then my shoes
   Would overflow with pearl,

Until we met the solid town.
   No one he seemed to know
And bowing with a mighty look
   At me, the sea withdrew.

EMILY DICKINSON

The Rime of the Ancient Mariner*

PART I

It is an ancient Mariner,
And he stoppeth one of three.
'By thy long grey beard and glittering eye,
Now wherefore stopp'st thou me?

The Bridegroom's doors are opened wide,
And I am next of kin;
The guests are met, the feast is set:
May'st hear the merry din.'

He holds him with his skinny hand,
'There was a ship,' quoth he.
'Hold off! unhand me, grey-beard loon!'
Eftsoons his hand dropt he.

He holds him with his glittering eye—
The Wedding-Guest stood still,
And listens like a three years' child:
The Mariner hath his will.

The Wedding-Guest sat on a stone:
He cannot choose but hear;
And thus spake on that ancient man,
The bright-eyed Mariner.

'The ship was cheered, the harbour cleared,
Merrily did we drop
Below the kirk, below the hill,
Below the lighthouse top.

The Sun came up upon the left,
Out of the sea came he!
And he shone bright, and on the right
Went down into the sea.

---

*This is a slightly shortened version of Coleridge's poem. Most of the omissions are
from the last three parts of the poem.

Higher and higher every day,
Till over the mast at noon—'
The Wedding-Guest here beat his breast,
For he heard the loud bassoon.

'And now the Storm-blast came, and he
Was tyrannous and strong:
He struck with his o'ertaking wings,
And chased us south along.

With sloping masts and dipping prow,
As who pursued with yell and blow
Still treads the shadow of his foe,
And forward bends his head,
The ship drove fast, loud roared the blast,
And southward aye we fled.

And now there came both mist and snow,
And it grew wondrous cold:
And ice, mast-high, came floating by,
As green as emerald.

And through the drifts the snowy clifts
Did send a dismal sheen:
Nor shapes of men nor beasts we ken—
The ice was all between.

The ice was here, the ice was there,
The ice was all around:
It cracked and growled, and roared and howled,
Like noises in a swound!

At length did cross an Albatross,
Thorough the fog it came;
As if it had been a Christian soul,
We hailed it in God's name.

It ate the food it ne'er had eat,
And round and round it flew.

The ice did split with a thunder-fit;
The helmsman steered us through!

And a good south wind sprung up behind;
The Albatross did follow,
And every day, for food or play,
Came to the mariners' hollo!

In mist or cloud, on mast or shroud,
It perched for vespers nine;
Whiles all the night, through fog-smoke white,
Glimmered the white moon-shine.'

'God save thee, ancient Mariner!
From the fiends, that plague thee thus!—
Why look'st thou so?'—'With my cross-bow
I shot the Albatross.'

PART II

'The Sun now rose upon the right:
Out of the sea came he,
Still hid in mist, and on the left
Went down into the sea.

And the good south wind still blew behind,
But no sweet bird did follow,
Nor any day for food or play
Come to the mariners' hollo!

And I had done a hellish thing,
And it would work 'em woe:
For all averred, I had killed the bird
That made the breeze to blow!
Ah wretch! said they, the bird to slay,
That made the breeze to blow!

Nor dim nor red, like God's own head,
The glorious Sun uprist:

Then all averred, I had killed the bird
That brought the fog and mist.
'Twas right, said they, such birds to slay,
That bring the fog and mist.

The fair breeze blew, the white foam flew,
The furrow followed free;
We were the first that ever burst
Into that silent sea.

Down dropt the breeze, the sails dropt down,
'Twas sad as sad could be;
And we did speak only to break
The silence of the sea!

All in a hot and copper sky,
The bloody Sun, at noon,
Right up above the mast did stand,
No bigger than the Moon.

Day after day, day after day,
We stuck, nor breath nor motion;
As idle as a painted ship
Upon a painted ocean.

Water, water, everywhere,
And all the boards did shrink;
Water, water, everywhere
Nor any drop to drink.

The very deep did rot: O Christ!
That ever this should be!
Yea, slimy things did crawl with legs
Upon the slimy sea.

About, about, in reel and rout
The death-fires danced at night;
The water, like a witch's oils,
Burnt, green and blue and white.

And some in dreams assured were
Of the Spirit that plagued us so;
Nine fathom deep he had followed us
From the land of mist and snow.

And every tongue, through utter drought,
Was withered at the root;
We could not speak, no more than if
We had been choked with soot.

Ah! well a-day! what evil looks
Had I from old and young!
Instead of the cross, the Albatross
About my neck was hung.'

PART III

'There passed a weary time. Each throat
Was parched, and glazed each eye.
A weary time! a weary time!
How glazed each weary eye,
When looking westward, I beheld
A something in the sky.

At first it seemed a little speck,
And then it seemed a mist;
It moved and moved, and took at last
A certain shape, I wist.

A speck, a mist, a shape, I wist!
And still it neared and neared:
As if it dodged a water-sprite,
It plunged and tacked and veered.

With throats unslaked, with black lips baked,
We could nor laugh nor wail;
Through utter drought all dumb we stood!
I bit my arm, I sucked the blood,
And cried, A sail! a sail!

With throats unslaked, with black lips baked,
Agape they heard me call:
Gramercy! they for joy did grin,
And all at once their breath drew in,
As they were drinking all.

See! see! (I cried) she tacks no more!
Hither to work us weal;
Without a breeze, without a tide,
She steadies with upright keel!

The western wave was all a-flame.
The day was well nigh done!
Almost upon the western wave
Rested the broad bright Sun;
When that strange shape drove suddenly
Betwixt us and the Sun.

And straight the Sun was flecked with bars,
(Heaven's Mother send us grace!)
As if through a dungeon-grate he peered
With broad and burning face.

Alas! (though I, and my heart beat loud)
How fast she nears and nears!
Are those her sails that glance in the Sun,
Like restless gossameres?

Are those her ribs through which the Sun
Did peer, as through a grate?
And is that Woman all her crew?
Is that a Death? and are there two?
Is Death that woman's mate?

Her lips were red, her looks were free,
Her locks were yellow as gold:
Her skin was as white as leprosy,
The Nightmare Life-in-Death was she,
Who thicks man's blood with cold.

The naked hulk alongside came,
And the twain were casting dice:
"The game is done! I've won! I've won,"
Quoth she, and whistles thrice.

The Sun's rim dips; the stars rush out:
At one stride comes the dark;
With far-heard whisper, o'er the sea,
Off shot the spectre-bark.

We listened and looked sideways up!
Fear at my heart, as at a cup,
My life-blood seemed to sip!
The stars were dim, and thick the night,
The steersman's face by his lamp gleamed white;
From the sails the dew did drip—
Till clomb above the eastern bar
The horned Moon, with one bright star
Within the nether tip.

One after one, by the star-dogged Moon,
Too quick for groan or sigh,
Each turned his face with a ghastly pang,
And cursed me with his eye.

Four times fifty living men,
(And I heard nor sigh nor groan)
With heavy thump, a lifeless lump,
They dropped down one by one.

The souls did from their bodies fly,—
They fled to bliss or woe!
And every soul, it passed me by,
Like the whizz of my cross-bow!'

PART IV

'I fear thee, ancient Mariner!
I fear thy skinny hand!

And thou art long, and lank, and brown,
As is the ribbed sea-sand.

I fear thee and thy glittering eye,
And thy skinny hand, so brown.'—
'Fear not, fear not, thou Wedding-Guest!
This body dropt not down.

Alone, alone, all, all alone,
Alone on a wide wide sea!
And never a saint took pity on
My soul in agony.

The many men, so beautiful!
And they all dead did lie:
And a thousand thousand slimy things
Lived on; and so did I.

I looked upon the rotting sea,
And drew my eyes away;
I looked upon the rotting deck,
And there the dead men lay.

I looked to heaven, and tried to pray;
But or ever a prayer had gusht,
A wicked whisper came, and made
My heart as dry as dust.

I closed my lids, and kept them close,
And the balls like pulses beat;
For the sky and the sea, and the sea and the sky
Lay like a load on my weary eye,
And the dead were at my feet.

The cold sweat melted from their limbs,
Nor rot nor reek did they:
The look with which they looked on me
Had never passed away.

An orphan's curse would drag to hell
A spirit from on high;
But oh! more horrible than that
Is the curse in a dead man's eye!
Seven days, seven nights, I saw that curse,
And yet I could not die.

The moving Moon went up the sky,
And no where did abide:
Softly she was going up,
And a star or two beside—

Her beams bemocked the sultry main,
Like April hoar-frost spread;
But where the ship's huge shadow lay,
The charmed water burnt alway
A still and awful red.

Beyond the shadow of the ship,
I watched the water-snakes:
They moved in tracks of shining white,
And when they reared, the elfish light
Fell off in hoary flakes.

Within the shadow of the ship
I watched their rich attire:
Blue, glossy green, and velvet black,
They coiled and swam; and every track
Was a flash of golden fire.

O happy living things! no tongue
Their beauty might declare:
A spring of love gushed from my heart,
And I blessed them unaware:
Sure my kind saint took pity on me,
And I blessed them unaware.

The self-same moment I could pray;
And from my neck so free

The Albatross fell off, and sank
Like lead into the sea.'

Part V

'Oh sleep! it is a gentle thing,
Beloved from pole to pole!
To Mary Queen the praise be given!
She sent the gentle sleep from Heaven,
That slid into my soul.

The silly buckets on the deck,
That had so long remained,
I dreamt that they were filled with dew;
And when I awoke, it rained.

My lips were wet, my throat was cold,
My garments all were dank;
Sure I had drunken in my dreams,
And still my body drank.

I moved, and could not feel my limbs:
I was so light— almost
I thought that I had died in sleep,
And was a blessed ghost.

And soon I heard a roaring wind:
It did not come anear;
But with its sound it shook the sails,
That were so thin and sere.

The loud wind never reached the ship,
Yet now the ship moved on!
Beneath the lightning and the Moon
The dead men gave a groan.

They groaned, they stirred, they all uprose,
Nor spake, nor moved their eyes:

It had been strange, even in a dream,
To have seen those dead men rise.

The helmsman steered, the ship moved on;
Yet never a breeze up-blew;
The mariners all 'gan work the ropes,
Where they were wont to do;
They raised their limbs like lifeless tools—
We were a ghastly crew.

The body of my brother's son
Stood by me, knee to knee:
The body and I pulled at one rope,
But he said nought to me.'

'I fear thee, ancient Mariner!'
'Be calm, thou Wedding-Guest!
'Twas not those souls that fled in pain,
Which to their corses came again,
But a troop of spirits blest:

For when it dawned—they dropped their arms,
And clustered round the mast;
Sweet sounds rose slowly through their mouths,
And from their bodies passed.

Till noon we quietly sailed on,
Yet never a breeze did breathe:
Slowly and smoothly went the ship,
Moved onward from beneath.

Under the keel nine fathom deep,
From the land of mist and snow,
The spirit slid: and it was he
That made the ship to go.
The sails at noon left off their tune,
And the ship stood still also.

The Sun, right up above the mast,
Had fixed her to the ocean:
But in a minute she 'gan stir,
With a short uneasy motion—
Backwards and forwards half her length
With a short uneasy motion.

Then like a pawing horse let go,
She made a sudden bound:
It flung the blood into my head,
And I fell down in a swound.

How long in that same fit I lay,
I have not to declare;
But ere my living life returned,
I heard and in my soul discerned
Two voices in the air.

"Is it he?" quoth one, "Is this the man?
By him who died on cross,
With his cruel bow he laid full low
The harmless Albatross.

The spirit who bideth by himself
In the land of mist and snow,
He loved the bird that loved the man
Who shot him with his bow."

The other was softer voice,
As soft as honey-dew:
Quoth he, "The man hath penance done,
And penance more will do."

PART VI

I woke and we were sailing on
As in a gentle weather:
'Twas night, calm night, the moon was high;
The dead men stood together.

All stood together on the deck,
For a charnel-dungeon fitter:
All fixed on me their stony eyes,
That in the Moon did glitter.

The pang, the curse, with which they died,
Had never passed away:
I could not draw my eyes from theirs,
Nor turn them up to pray.

But soon there breathed a wind on me,
Nor sound nor motion made:
Its path was not upon the sea,
In ripple or in shade.

It raised my hair, it fanned my cheek
Like a meadow-gale of spring—
It mingled strangely with my fears,
Yet it felt like a welcoming.

Swiftly, swiftly flew the ship,
Yet she sailed softly too:
Sweetly, sweetly blew the breeze—
On me alone it blew.

Oh! dream of joy! is this indeed
The light-house top I see?
Is this the hill? is this the kirk?
Is this mine own countree?

We drifted o'er the harbour-bar,
And I with sobs did pray—
O let me be awake, my God!
Or let me sleep alway.

The harbour-bay was clear as glass,
So smoothly it was strewn!
And on the bay the moonlight lay,
And the shadow of the Moon.

The rock shone bright, the kirk no less,
That stands above the rock:
The moonlight steeped in silentness
The steady weathercock.

And the bay was white with silent light,
Till rising from the same,
Full many shapes, that shadows were,
In crimson colours came.

A little distance from the prow
Those crimson shadows were:
I turned my eyes upon the deck—
Oh, Christ! what saw I there!

Each corse lay flat, lifeless and flat,
And, by the holy rood!
A man all light, a seraph-man,
On every corse there stood,

This seraph-band, each waved his hand:
It was a heavenly sight!
They stood as signals to the land,
Each one a lovely light;

This seraph-band, each waved his hand,
No voice did they impart—
No voice; but oh! the silence sank
Like music on my heart.

But soon I heard the dash of oars.
I heard the Pilot's cheer;
My head was turned perforce away
And I saw a boat appear.

The Pilot and the Pilot's boy,
I heard them coming fast:
Dear Lord in Heaven! it was a joy
The dead men could not blast.

I saw a third—I heard his voice:
It is the Hermit good!
He singeth loud his godly hymns
That he makes in the wood.
He'll shrieve my soul, he'll wash away
The Albatross's blood.'

PART VII

'This Hermit good lives in that wood
Which slopes down to the sea.
How loudly his sweet voice he rears!
He loves to talk with marineres
That come from a far countree.

The skiff-boat neared: I heard them talk,
"Why, this is strange, I trow!
Where are those lights so many and fair,
That signal made but now?"

"Strange, by my faith!" the Hermit said—
"And they answered not our cheer!
The planks looked warped! and see those sails,
How thin they are and sere!"

"Dear Lord! it hath a fiendish look"—
(The Pilot made reply)
"I am a-feared"—"Push on, push on!"
Said the Hermit cheerily.

The boat came closer to the ship.
But I nor spake nor stirred;
The boat came close beneath the ship,
And straight a sound was heard.

Under the water it rumbled on,
Still louder and more dread:
It reached the ship, it split the bay;
The ship went down like lead.

Stunned by that loud and dreadful sound,
Which sky and ocean smote,
Like one that hath been seven days drowned
My body lay afloat;
But swift as dreams, myself I found
Within the Pilot's boat.

Upon the whirl, where sank the ship,
The boat spun round and round;
And all was still, save that the hill
Was telling of the sound.

I moved my lips—the Pilot shrieked
And fell down in a fit;
The holy Hermit raised his eyes,
And prayed where he did sit.

I took the oars: the Pilot's boy,
Who now doth crazy go,
Laughed loud and long, and all the while
His eyes went to and fro.
"Ha! ha!" quoth he, "full plain I see,
The Devil knows how to row."

And now, all in my own countree,
I stood on the firm land!
The Hermit stepped forth from the boat,
And scarcely he could stand.

"O shrieve me, shrieve me, holy man!"
The Hermit crossed his brow.
"Say quick," quoth he, "I bid thee say—
What manner of man art thou?"

Forthwith this frame of mine was wrenched
With a woful agony,
Which forced me to begin my tale;
And then it left me free.

Since then, at an uncertain hour,
That agony returns:
And till my ghastly tale is told,
This heart within me burns.

I pass, like night, from land to land;
I have strange power of speech;
That moment that his face I see,
I know the man that must hear me:
To him my tale I teach.

O Wedding-Guest! this soul hath been
Alone on a wide wide sea:
So lonely 'twas, that God himself
Scarce seemed there to be.

Farewell, farewell! but this I tell
To thee, thou Wedding-Guest!
He prayeth well, who loveth well
Both man and bird and beast.

He prayeth best, who loveth best
All things both great and small;
For the dear God who loveth us,
He made and loveth all.'

The Mariner, whose eye is bright,
Whose beard with age is hoar,
Is gone: and now the Wedding Guest
Turned from the bridegroom's door.

He went like one that hath been stunned,
And is of sense forlorn:
A sadder and a wiser man,
He rose the morrow morn.

S. T. COLERIDGE

Casey Jones

Come all you rounders if you want to hear
The story of a brave engineer;
Casey Jones was the hogger's name,
On a big eight-wheeler, boys, he won his fame.
Caller called Casey at half-past four,
He kissed his wife at the station door,
Mounted to the cabin with orders in his hand,
And took his farewell trip to the promised land.

   Casey Jones, he mounted to the cabin,
   Casey Jones, with his order in his hand!
   Casey Jones, he mounted to the cabin,
   Took his farewell trip into the promised land.

Put in your water and shovel in your coal,
Put your head out the window, watch the drivers roll,
I'll run her till she leaves the rail,
'Cause we're eight hours late with the Western Mail!
He looked at his watch and his watch was slow,
Looked at the water and the water was low,
Turned to his fireboy and said,
'We'll get to 'Frisco, but we'll all be dead!'

                                             (*Refrain*)

Casey pulled up Reno Hill,
Tooted for the crossing with an awful shrill,
Snakes all knew by the engine's moans
That the hogger at the throttle was Casey Jones.
He pulled up short two miles from the place,
Number Four stared him right in the face,
Turned to his fireboy, said 'You'd better jump,
'Cause there's two locomotives that's going to bump!'

                                             (*Refrain*)

Casey said, just before he died,
'There's two more roads I'd like to ride.'
Fireboy said, 'What can they be?'
'The Rio Grande and the old SP.'
Mrs Jones sat on her bed a-sighing,
Got a pink that Casey was dying,
Said, 'Go to bed, children; hush your crying,
'Cause you've got another papa on the Salt Lake Line.'

   Casey Jones! Got another papa!
   Casey Jones, on the Salt Lake Line!
   Casey Jones! Got another papa!
   Got another papa on the Salt Lake Line!

ANON.

The Lion and Albert

There's a famous seaside place called Blackpool,
    That's noted for fresh air and fun,
And Mr and Mrs Ramsbottom
    Went there with young Albert, their son.

A grand little lad was young Albert,
    All dressed in his best; quite a swell
With a stick with an 'orse's 'ead 'andle,
    The finest that Woolworth's could sell.

They didn't think much to the Ocean:
    The waves, they was fiddlin' and small,
There was no wrecks and nobody drownded,
    Fact, nothing to laugh at at all.

So, seeking for further amusement,
    They paid and went into the Zoo,
Where they'd Lions and Tigers and Camels,
    And old ale and sandwiches too.

There were one great big Lion called Wallace;
    His nose were all covered with scars
He lay in a somnolent posture,
    With the side of his face on the bars.

Now Albert had heard about Lions,
    How they was ferocious and wild
To see Wallace lying so peaceful,
    Well, it didn't seem right to the child.

So straightway the brave little feller,
    Not showing a morsel of fear,
Took his stick with its 'orse's 'ead 'andle
    And pushed it in Wallace's ear.

You could see that the Lion didn't like it,
    For giving a kind of a roll,

He pulled Albert inside the cage with 'im,
  And swallowed the little lad 'ole.

Then Pa, who had seen the occurrence,
  And didn't know what to do next,
Said 'Mother! Yon Lion's 'et Albert',
  And Mother said 'Well, I am vexed!'

Then Mr and Mrs Ramsbottom
  Quite rightly, when all's said and done,
Complained to the Animal Keeper,
  That the Lion had eaten their son.

The keeper was quite nice about it;
  He said 'What a nasty mishap.
Are you sure that it's *your* boy he's eaten?'
  Pa said 'Am I sure? There's his cap!'

The manager had to be sent for.
  He came and he said 'What's to do?'
Pa said 'Yon Lion's 'et Albert,
  And 'im in his Sunday clothes, too.'

Then Mother said, 'Right's right, young feller;
  I think it's a shame and a sin,
For a lion to go and eat Albert,
  And after we've paid to come in.'

The manager wanted no trouble,
  He took out his purse right away,
Saying 'How much to settle the matter?'
  And Pa said 'What do you usually pay?'

But Mother had turned a bit awkward
  When she thought where her Albert had gone.
She said 'No! someone's got to be summonsed'—
  So that was decided upon.

Then off they went to the P'lice Station,
    In front of the Magistrate chap;
They told 'im what happened to Albert,
    And proved it by showing his cap.

The Magistrate gave his opinion
    That no one was really to blame
And he said that he hoped the Ramsbottoms
    Would have further sons to their name.

At that Mother got proper blazing,
    'And thank you, sir, kindly,' said she.
'What waste all our lives raising children
    To feed ruddy Lions? Not me!'

MARRIOTT EDGAR

Ballad of the Bread Man

Mary stood in the kitchen
    Baking a loaf of bread.
An angel flew in through the window.
    'We've a job for you,' he said.

'God in his big gold heaven,
    Sitting in his big blue chair,
Wanted a mother for his little son.
    Suddenly saw you there.'

Mary shook and trembled,
    'It isn't true what you say.'
'Don't say that,' said the angel.
    'The baby's on its way.'

Joseph was in the workshop
    Planing a piece of wood.
'The old man's past it,' the neighbours said.
    'That girl's been up to no good.'

'And who was that elegant fellow,'
    They said, 'in the shiny gear?'
The things they said about Gabriel
    Were hardly fit to hear.

Mary never answered,
    Mary never replied.
She kept the information,
    Like the baby, safe inside.

It was election winter.
    They went to vote in town.
When Mary found her time had come
    The hotels let her down.

The baby was born in an annexe
    Next to the local pub.
At midnight, a delegation
    Turned up from the Farmers' Club.

They talked about an explosion
    That made a hole in the sky,
Said they'd been sent to the Lamb & Flag
    To see God come down from on high.

A few days later a bishop
    And a five-star general were seen
With the head of an African country
    In a bullet-proof limousine.

'We've come,' they said, 'with tokens
    For the little boy to choose.'
Told the tale about war and peace
    In the television news.

After them came the soldiers
    With rifle and bomb and gun,
Looking for enemies of the state.
    The family had packed and gone.

When they got back to the village
　　The neighbours said, to a man,
'That boy will never be one of us,
　　Though he does what he blessed well can.'

He went round to all the people
　　A paper crown on his head.
Here is some bread from my father.
　　Take, eat, he said.

Nobody seemed very hungry.
　　Nobody seemed to care.
Nobody saw the god in himself
　　Quietly standing there.

He finished up in the papers.
　　He came to a very bad end.
He was charged with bringing the living to life.
　　No man was that prisoner's friend.

There's only one kind of punishment
　　To fit that kind of a crime.
They rigged a trial and shot him dead.
　　They were only just in time.

They lifted the young man by the leg,
　　They lifted him by the arm,
They locked him in a cathedral
　　In case he came to harm.

They stored him safe as water
　　Under seven rocks.
One Sunday morning he burst out
　　Like a jack-in-the-box.

Through the town he went walking.
　　He showed them the holes in his head.
Now do you want any loaves? he cried.
　　'Not today,' they said.

CHARLES CAUSLEY

★ **Performing** — *Casey Jones* is a song about the driver of one of the great railway engines in the days of the Wild West. You can rehearse a rousing performance of the piece by splitting the eight line verses into two sets of four lines and giving them to different voices. Of course, everybody joins in the refrain.

— *The Lion and Albert* was a famous party piece of years ago. You can dramatise it by having different people take the different parts—the Narrator, Mr and Mrs Ramsbottom, the Keeper and the Manager.

— *Ballad of the Breadman* is on an altogether more serious subject than the other two pieces though it seems very jokey at first. Hear it read through first and, in small groups, talk through what you think it is saying. When you are fairly sure you have the feel of the poem, divide up the story between different voices and perform the poem.

— *The Ancient Mariner* is probably one of the longest poems you have come across. First, try to get to know the whole story. You might:

(i) Prepare a reading of the poem, live or taped. It's probably best to tackle this as a serial in three instalments:

Parts 1–3 journey out— killing the albatross—the spectre ship
—death of the sailors.
Parts 4–5 mariner's isolation—blessing water snakes—ghosts of sailors work the ship—Polar Spirit speeds ship to Northern waters
Parts 6–7 journey back—angels over the corpses of the sailors —met by the Pilot and the Hermit—ship sinks in the harbour—mariner's life of constant penance.

(ii) Try to hear a recording, e.g. LP record *Coleridge* PLP1039 Argo/Decca.

(iii) Find a copy of *The Rime of the Ancient Mariner*, illustrated by Gustav Doré (Dover/Constable paperback). This has the full text, an outline of the events alongside the poem and 40 powerful illustrations which will help you to follow the story. (We have reproduced a few on a smaller scale here.)

(iv) Next, map the voyage. Make a frieze or illustrated map showing the mariner's progress. Perhaps groups could work on different sections of the poem. Alongside the illustrations you could:

copy out suitable lines or verses from the poem;
invent a ship's log;
write the mariner's diary.

(v) There are other ways of bringing the poem alive, for example:
Movement. Choose a short episode from the poem—e.g. the mariner's meeting with the wedding guest, killing the albatross and the changing reactions of the sailors, the dead men working the ropes—and, in groups, work out a mime or tableau to accompany the reading of the extract.

Mural. A group could create a single, large picture to show the main events that happen at the three levels—air, sea, under-water. Make it a three-tiered design, perhaps with one main colour for each tier.

Message. Write the mariner's message in a bottle. Decide where he is (probably somewhere distant in Parts 5 or 6) and write his description of what's happened and his plea for help.

Nonsense and Stuff

The Two Old Bachelors

Two old Bachelors were living in one house;
One caught a Muffin, the other caught a Mouse.
Said he who caught the Muffin to him who caught the
    Mouse,—
'This happens just in time! For we've nothing in the house,
'Save a tiny slice of lemon and a teaspoonful of honey,
'And what to do for dinner—since we haven't any money?
'And what can we expect if we haven't any dinner,
'But to lose our teeth and eyelashes and keep on growing
    thinner?'

Said he who caught the Mouse to him who caught the
    Muffin,—
'We might cook this little Mouse, if we only had some
    Stuffin'!
'If we had but Sage and Onion we could do extremely well,
'But how to get that Stuffin' it is difficult to tell!'

Those two old Bachelors ran quickly to the town
And asked for Sage and Onion as they wandered up and
    down;
They borrowed two large Onions, but no Sage was to be
    found
In the Shops, or in the Market, or in all the Gardens round.

But some one said,—'A hill there is, a little to the north,
'And to its purpledicular top a narrow way leads forth;—

'And there among the rugged rocks abides an ancient
    Sage,—
'An earnest Man, who reads all day a most perplexing page.

'Climb up, and seize him by the toes!—all studious as he
    sits,—
'And pull him down,—and chop him into endless little bits!
'Then mix him with your Onion (cut up likewise into
    Scraps),—
'When your Stuffin' will be ready—and very good: perhaps.'

Those two old Bachelors without loss of time
The nearly purpledicular crags at once began to climb;
And at the top, among the rocks, all seated in a nook,
They saw that Sage, a-reading of a most enormous book.
'You earnest Sage!' aloud they cried, 'your book you've read
    enough in!—
'We wish to chop you into bits to mix you into Stuffin'!'

But that old Sage looked calmly up, and with his awful book,
At those two Bachelors' bald heads a certain aim he took;—
And over Crag and precipice they rolled promiscuous
    down,—
At once they rolled, and never stopped in lane or field or
    town,—
And when they reached their house, they found (beside
    their want of Stuffin'),
The Mouse had fled;—and, previously, had eaten up the
    Muffin.

They left their home in silence by the once convivial door,
And from that hour those Bachelors were never heard of
    more.

                                        EDWARD LEAR

Forth From His Den

Forth from his den to steal he stole.
His bag of chink he chunk,
And many a wicked smile he smole,
And many a wink he wunk.

ANON.

The Hunter

The hunter crouches in his blind
'Neath camouflage of every kind,
And conjures up a quacking noise
To lend allure to his decoys.
This grown-up man, with pluck and luck,
Is hoping to outwit a duck.

OGDEN NASH

The Eel

I don't mind eels
Except as meals.
And the way they feels.

OGDEN NASH

The Termite

Some primal termite knocked on wood
And tasted it, and found it good,
And that is why your cousin May
Fell through the parlor floor today.

OGDEN NASH

The Firefly

The firefly's flame
Is something for which science has no name.
I can think of nothing eerier
Than flying around with an unidentified glow on a person's
    posteerier.

OGDEN NASH

Three Limericks

There was an old fellow of Tring
Who, when somebody asked him to sing,
    Replied, 'Ain't it odd?
    I can never tell *God*
Save the Weasel from *Pop goes the King*.'

ANON.

There was an old man from Darjeeling,
Who boarded a bus bound for Ealing.
    He saw on the door:
    'Please don't spit on the floor',
So he stood up and spat on the ceiling.

ANON.

There was an old man from Dunoon,
Who always ate soup with a fork,
    For he said, 'As I eat
    Neither fish, fowl nor flesh,
I should finish my dinner too quick.'

ANON.

Unemployable

'I usth thu workth in the thircusth,'
He said,
Between the intermittent showers that emerged from his
    mouth.
'Oh,' I said, 'what did you do?'
'I usth thu catcth bulleth in my theeth.'

GARETH OWEN

The Stern Parent

Father heard his Children scream,
So he threw them in the stream,
Saying, as he drowned the third,
'Children should be seen, *not* heard!'

HARRY GRAHAM

Appreciation

Auntie did you feel no pain
   Falling from that willow tree?
Will you do it, please, again?
   Cos my friend here didn't see.

HARRY GRAHAM

Tender-Heartedness

Billy, in one of his nice new sashes,
Fell in the fire and was burnt to ashes
Now, although the room grows chilly,
I haven't the heart to poke poor Billy.

HARRY GRAHAM

When you're a GROWN-UP

When you're a GROWN-UP
a SERIOUS and SENSIBLE PERSON
When you've stopped being SILLY
you can go out and have babies
and go into a SERIOUS and SENSIBLE shop
and ask for:
Tuftytails, Paddipads, Bikkipegs, Cosytoes
and
Tommy Tippee Teethers.
Sno-bunnies, Visivents, Safeshines
Comfybaths, Dikkybibs
and
Babywipes.
Rumba Rattles and Trigger Jiggers
A Whirlee Three, a Finger Flip
or A Quacky Duck.
And if you're very SENSIBLE
you can choose
Easifitz, Baby buggies and a Safesitterstand.
Or is it a
Saferstandsit?
No it's a Sitstandsafe. I can never remember.
I'm sorry but Babytalk is a very difficult
    language.
It's for adults only.
Like 'X' films
Much too horrible for children.

MICHAEL ROSEN

Queeriflora Babyöides

119

You Tell Me

Here are the football results:
League Division Fun
Manchester United won, Manchester City lost.
Crystal Palace 2, Buckingham Palace 1
Millwall Leeds nowhere
Wolves 8 A cheese roll and had a cup of tea 2
Aldershot 3 Buffalo Bill shot 2
Evertonill, Liverpool's not very well either
Newcastle's Heaven Sunderland's a very nice place 2
Ipswich one? You tell me.

MICHAEL ROSEN

Silly Old Baboon

There was a Baboon
Who, one afternoon,
Said, 'I think I will fly to the sun.'
So, with two great palms
Strapped to his arms,
He started his take-off run.

Mile after mile
He galloped in style
But never once left the ground.
'You're running too slow,'
Said a passing crow,
'Try reaching the speed of sound.'

So he put on a spurt—
By God how it hurt!
The soles of his feet caught fire.
There were great clouds of steam
As he raced through a stream
But he still didn't get any higher.

Racing on through the night,
Both his knees caught alight
And smoke billowed out from his rear.
Quick to his aid
Came a fire brigade
Who chased him for over a year.

Many moons passed by.
Did Baboon every fly?
Did he ever get to the sun?
I've just heard today
That he's well on his way!
He'll be passing through Acton at one.

PS Well, what do you expect from a Baboon?

SPIKE MILLIGAN

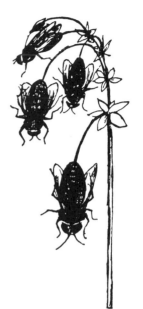

Bluebottlia Buzztilentia

Tigerlillia Terribilis

121

The Vandalingo

In the rotting lake called Albion
That's thick as kedgeree
Lurks the odious Vandalingo
With his scurvy wife Debris.

Beneath a mildewed, rusting gas fire
Near an old bike and a plank
The Vandalingo makes his home
In a waste disposal tank.

His carcass smells of Wellingtons
His boots are size fifteen
His nails leak inky messages
To his baby son Globscene.

His teeth are broken hacksaw blades
His lips drip kerosene
He belches fumes and poison gas
From his lungs of polythene.

For years he sleeps his dreamless sleeps
Amongst rusting beds and cars
But then one night he rises up
To sport beneath the stars.

And then through webs of rotting weeds
Two spinning fog lamps loom
As the Vandalingo's yellow eyes
Peer dimly through the gloom.

The surface of the rotting lake
Lifts like a tent of slime
As the Vandalingo crashes through
To chant his ancient rhyme.

'Tonight I vandalinger
And though I'm rarely seen

From the broken trail I leave behind
You'll know where I have been.

'I crash through walls and hedges
I uproot flowers and trees
I spread garbage, swill and bacon rind
Where they're sure to cause disease.

'I scrawl my name on subway walls
I chew the seats on trains
I hurl prams and bottles into ponds
And my head through window panes.'

And if your school's been flooded
And there's ink down every wall
You can be sure that sometime in the night
The Vandalingo's called.

As dawn creeps up the city streets
He drags home 'neath the moon's pale stare
And in a belch of bubbling mud
Sinks gurgling to his lair.

And there he's joyfully welcomed
By Globscene and his spouse Debris
And to the waking world above
They wail this song of glee.

'We are the Vandalingos
There's but one thought in our brain
That though we sleep ten thousand years
Our time will come again.'

GARETH OWEN

Three Parodies

While shepherds watched their turnip tops
   All boiling in the pot,
A lump of soot came rolling down
   And spoilt the bloomin' lot.

ANON.

We three kings of Orient are
One in a taxi, one in a car,
One on a scooter blowing his hooter
Following yonder star.

ANON.

Good King Wenceslas looked out
   On the Feast of Stephen;
A snowball hit him on the snout
   And made it all uneven.
Brightly shone his conk that night
   Though the pain was cruel,
Till the doctor came in sight
   Riding on a mu-oo-el.

ANON.

From Hiawatha

   Swift of foot was Hiawatha;
He could shoot an arrow from him,
And run forward with such fleetness
That the arrow fell behind him!
Strong of arm was Hiawatha;
He could shoot ten arrows upward,
Shoot them with such strength and swiftness,
That the tenth had left the bowstring
Ere the first to earth had fallen!
   He had mittens, Minjekahwun,
Magic mittens made of deer-skin.
When upon his hands he wore them,

He could smite the rocks asunder,
He could grind them into powder.
He had moccasins enchanted,
Magic moccasins of deer-skin;
When he bound them round his ankles,
When upon his feet he tied them,
At each stride a mile he measured!

H. W. LONGFELLOW

The Modern Hiawatha

When he killed the Mudjokivis,
Of the skin he made him mittens,
Made them with the fur side inside,
Made them with the skin side outside,
He, to get the warm side inside,
Put the inside skin side outside.
He, to get the cold side outside,
Put the warm side fur side inside,
That's why he put the fur side inside,
Why he put the skin side outside,
Why he turned them inside outside.

ANON.

★ **Do It Yourself.** Limericks aren't too difficult to write if you listen carefully to their rhythm and get the rhyming pattern right. The first, second and fifth lines rhyme with each other and so do the shorter third and fourth lines. (The third limerick on p. 116 obstinately refuses to rhyme but you can work out what words would make it fit the pattern.)

—Have a go at a limerick yourself, perhaps starting in the time-honoured way 'There was a young lady/old man/etc. from . . .'.

—*Ruthless Rhymes* is the title Harry Graham gave to his four line verses like *Tender-Heartedness*, *Appreciation* and *The Stern Parent* which you will find on p. 117. They have two pairs of rhyming lines and have to be very unkind. Can you compose your own *Ruthless Rhyme* and draw a picture to go with it?

★ **Parodies.** Everybody knows one or two parodies. Generations of children have sung the wrong words (sometimes the rude words) to serious carols and hymns such as those on p. 124. Do you know any others? The parody of *Hiawatha* on p. 125 is one example. More difficult—try writing your own parody of a well-known verse.

★ **Performing** —Edward Lear's story of *The Two Old Bachelors* on p. 113 can be turned into a lively tape-recording or be acted out by a small group. For your cast you need a narrator, the two old bachelors, the person who gives them directions and, of course, the Sage.

—Even Gareth Owen's five line poem *Unemployable* can be performed. It needs a narrator for lines two and three, a speaker for line four and the bullet catcher for the first and last lines. Although it's short, it will need very careful rehearsal to get the timing and expression right.

—Michael Rosen's poem *When You're a Grown-Up* can be performed by having 'a very serious and sensible person' as narrator to begin the poem and then lots of different voices each saying the name of one of the babythings. The narrator could come in with the word 'and' at lines 8 and 12; he could also say lines 17 and 18 and the last seven lines. Again the timing is tricky, so you will need to rehearse. Practise by using a tape-recorder.

—Have you noticed how the tone of the sports reporter's voice usually tells you what the football result is before the sentence is even finished? If the reporter's tone rises when naming the first team and goes down when naming the second, you know the first team has won. If the result is the other way round the tones are reversed: and, of course, a draw is announced with level tones for both teams. Try to read Michael Rosen's *You Tell Me* using the right tones and being quite serious.

—Gareth Owen's poem about the vandalous *Vandalingo* (p. 122) can be read by four voices—the narrator and the Vandalingo share most of the poem but the disgusting Debris and Globscene can join in the chorus of the last verse.

—The parody of Longfellow's poem *Hiawatha* on p. 125 is a very tricky tongue-twister. Practise until you can say it without tripping yourself up. A small group of you can try speaking it in chorus or split the poem into pairs of lines for four main voices with everybody solemnly joining in for the last three lines.

Weather

Whatever the weather

Whether the weather be fine, or whether the weather be not,
Whether the weather be cold, or whether the weather be hot,
We'll weather the weather, whatever the weather,
   Whether we like it or not.

ANON.

Early Rain

After the long drought
The sun goes quickly out.
Leaf after leaf in the laden trees
Like cats' ears flick.
Dusty flowers on a dry stick
Stagger beneath the blows
Of the downpour breeze.
Each tree is a sounding drum,
And every rose
Is trampled in the hum
Of the shower's watery bees.

JAMES KIRKUP

Winter-piece

You wake, all windows blind—embattled sprays
grained on the medieval glass.
Gates snap like gunshot
as you handle them. Five-barred fragility
sets flying fifteen rooks who go together
silently ravenous above this winter-piece
that will not feed them. They alight
beyond, scavenging, missing everything
but the bladed atmosphere, the white resistance.
Ruts with iron flanges track
through a hard decay
where you discern once more
oak-leaf by hawthorn, for the frost
rewhets their edges. In a perfect web
blanched along each spoke
and circle of its woven wheel,
the spider hangs, grasp unbroken
and death-masked in cold. Returning
you see the house glint-out behind
its holed and ragged glaze,
frost-fronds all streaming.

CHARLES TOMLINSON

Hard Frost

Frost called to water 'Halt!'
And crusted the moist snow with sparkling salt;
Brooks, their own bridges, stop,
And icicles in long stalactites drop,
And tench in water-holes
Lurk under gluey glass like fish in bowls.

In the hard-rutted lane
At every footstep breaks a brittle pane,
And tinkling trees ice-bound,
Changed into weeping willows, sweep the ground;
Dead boughs take root in ponds
And ferns on windows shoot their ghostly fronds.

But vainly the fierce frost
Interns poor fish, ranks trees in an armed host,
Hangs daggers from house-eaves
And on the windows ferny ambush weaves;
In the long war grown warmer
The sun will strike him dead and strip his armour.

ANDREW YOUNG

Winter Days

Biting air
Winds blow
City streets
Under snow

Noses red
Lips sore
Runny eyes
Hands raw

Chimneys smoke
Cars crawl
Piled snow
On garden wall

Slush in gutters
Ice in lanes
Frosty patterns
On window panes

Morning call
Lift up head
Nipped by winter
Stay in bed

GARETH OWEN

Snow

Ridged thickly on black bough
  And foaming on twig-fork in swollen lumps
At flirt of bird-wing or wind's sough
  Plump snow tumbled on snow softly with sudden dumps.

Where early steps had made
  A wavering track through the white-blotted road
Breaking its brightness with blue shade,
  Snow creaked beneath my feet with snow heavily shod.

I reached a snow-thatched rick
  Where men sawed bedding off for horse and cow;
There varnished straws were lying thick
  Paving with streaky gold the trodden silver snow.

Such light filled me with awe,
  And nothing marred my paradisal thought,
That robin least of all I saw
  Lying too fast asleep, his song choked in his throat.

ANDREW YOUNG

Fog

The fog comes
on little cat feet.

It sits looking
over harbour and city
on silent haunches
and then moves on.

CARL SANDBURG

Mist

Subtle as an illusionist
The deft hands of the morning mist
Play tricks upon my sight:
Haystacks dissolve and hedges lift
Out of the unseen fields and drift
Between the veils of white.

On the horizon, heads of trees
Swim with the mist about their knees,
And when the farm dogs bark,
I turn to watch how on the calm
Of that white sea, the red-roofed farm
Floats like a Noah's Ark.

DOUGLAS GIBSON

Storm in the Black Forest

Now it is almost night, from the bronzey soft sky
jugfull after jugfull of pure white liquid fire, bright white
tipples over and spills down,
and is gone
and gold-bronze flutters bent through the thick upper air.

And as the electric liquid pours out, sometimes
a still brighter white snake wriggles among it, spilled
and tumbling wriggling down the sky:
and then the heavens cackle with uncouth sounds.

And the rain won't come, the rain refuses to come!

This is the electricity that man is supposed to have mastered,
chained, subjugated to his use!
supposed to!

D. H. LAWRENCE

A Storm

Somebody is throttling that tree
By the way it's threshing about;
I'm glad it's no one I know, or me,
The head thrust back at the throat,

Green hair tumbled and cracking throat.
His thumbs drive into her windpipe,
She cannot cry out,
Only swishing and groaning: death swells ripe,

The light is dimming but the fight goes on.
Chips strike my window. In the morning, there
Stands the tree, still, bushy and calm,
Not as I saw it, twisted heel to ear,

But fluffed up, boughs chafing slightly.
What's become of her attacker?
I'm glad he's not mine or known to me,
Flipped to the ground, heel over ear:

She preens herself, with a soft bough-purr.
Was he swallowed up, lip over ear?
He's gone anyway. The path is thick in her fur.
Am I a friend, may I walk near?

PETER REDGROVE

A Hot Day

Cottonwool clouds loiter.
A lawnmower, very far,
Birrs. Then a bee comes
To a crimson rose and softly,
Deftly and fatly crams
A velvet body in.

A tree, June-lazy, makes
A tent of dim green light.
Sunlight weaves in the leaves,
Honey-light laced with leaf light,
Green interleaved with gold.
Sunlight gathers its rays
In sheaves, which the wind unweaves
And then reweaves—the wind
That puffs a smell of grass
Through the heat-heavy, trembling
Summer pool of air.

A. S. J. TESSIMOND

★ **Performing** —A group could prepare a reading, live or taped, of the poems *Whatever the Weather* (p. 127), *Winter Days* (p. 130) and *A Hot Day* (p. 135). As you rehearse, try to suggest the contrast between hot and cold weather in the tones of the voices you choose and the pace of the reading. You may decide to start and finish your performance with *Whatever the Weather*; *Winter Days* could be spoken with a fresh voice every two lines; *A Hot Day* could be shared between two voices, one for each section.

★ **Writing** —List poems. Make a list of the things that you associate with each of the four seasons. Begin your lists 'Summer is . . .', 'Autumn is . . .' etc., and start a fresh line for each item. Either, illustrate your own list poems or, with the rest of the class, make up a wall display of poems and pictures on the theme of the seasons. Alternatively, each of you could contribute one line to a class poem.
—Comparisons. 'The fog comes/on little cat feet' (p. 132); lightning is seen as a wriggling 'white snake' (p. 133); frozen earth has 'ruts with iron flanges' (p. 128). Choose *one* aspect of the weather and try to capture it in a brief word-picture—no more than a few lines like the poem *Fog* on p. 132. If you can find a comparison, so much the better.
—Haiku Yearbook. The aim here is to make a series of twelve short descriptions, one for each month of the year. A haiku poem has 17 syllables, arranged 5–7–5 over three lines. Share out the months and write and illustrate your 'yearbook'.
—Pictures into poems. The photograph on p. 130 shows a street-corner scene which may remind you of bleak, wintry days in town. Can you find words to describe the way snow sticks to coats, road-signs and pillars and affects roads and pavements? What do you notice about the way people stand? What details tell you that there is a strong wind driving the snow? What do you imagine the people's feelings to be? You may be able to write a poem suggested by the picture.
—Weather forecast. 'Here is the forecast for the coming week . . .
   Monday will be muggy, murky . . .
   Tuesday will be tempests, typhoons, tornadoes . . .
   Wednesday will be . . .'
Work in groups to invent a nonsense weather forecast. When it's complete, share out the lines and prepare a live reading for the rest of the class.

Dreams and Hauntings

The Very Image

An image of my grandmother
her head appearing upside-down upon a cloud
the cloud transfixed on the steeple
of a deserted railway-station
far away

An image of an aqueduct
with a dead crow hanging from the first arch
a modern-style chair from the second
a fir-tree lodged in the third
and the whole scene sprinkled with snow

An image of the piano-tuner
with a basket of prawns on his shoulder
and a firescreen under his arm
his moustache made of clay-clotted twigs
and his cheeks daubed with wine

An image of an aeroplane
the propeller is rashers of bacon
the wings are of reinforced lard
the tail is made of paper-clips
the pilot is a wasp

An image of the painter
with his left hand in a bucket
and his right hand stroking a cat
as he lies in bed
with a stone beneath his head

And all these images
and many others
are arranged like waxworks
in model bird-cages
about six inches high.

DAVID GASCOYNE

Night-fright

There was a young lady called Wemyss,
Who, it semyss, was troubled with dremyss.
   She would wake in the night
   And, in terrible fright,
Shake the bemyss of the house with her scremyss.

ANON.

Kubla Khan

In Xanadu did Kubla Khan
A stately pleasure-dome decree:
Where Alph, the sacred river, ran
Through caverns measureless to man
   Down to a sunless sea.
So twice five miles of fertile ground
With walls and towers were girdled round:
And there were gardens bright with sinuous rills,
Where blossomed many an incense-bearing tree;
And here were forests ancient as the hills,
Enfolding sunny spots of greenery.
But oh! that deep romantic chasm which slanted
Down the green hill athwart a cedarn cover!
A savage place! as holy and enchanted
As e'er beneath a waning moon was haunted
By woman wailing for her demon-lover!
And from this chasm, with ceaseless turmoil seething,
As if this earth in fast thick pants were breathing,
A mighty fountain momently was forced:
Amid whose swift half-intermitted burst
Huge fragments vaulted like rebounding hail,
Or chaffy grain beneath the thresher's flail:
And 'mid these dancing rocks at once and ever
It flung up momently the sacred river.
Five miles meandering with a mazy motion
Through wood and dale the sacred river ran,
Then reached the caverns measureless to man,
And sank in tumult to a lifeless ocean:
And 'mid this tumult Kubla heard from far
Ancestral voices prophesying war!

   The shadow of the dome of pleasure
   Floated midway on the waves;
   Where was heard the mingled measure
   From the fountain and the caves.
It was a miracle of rare device,
A sunny pleasure-dome with caves of ice!

A damsel with a dulcimer
In a vision once I saw:
It was an Abyssinian maid,
And on her dulcimer she played,
Singing of Mount Abora.
Could I revive within me
Her symphony and song,
To such a deep delight 'twould win me,
That with music loud and long,
I would build that dome in air,
That sunny dome! those caves of ice!
And all who heard should see them there,
And all should cry, Beware! Beware!
His flashing eyes, his floating hair!
Weave a circle round him thrice,
And close your eyes with holy dread,
For he on honey-dew hath fed,
And drunk the milk of Paradise.

S. T. COLERIDGE

The Nightmare

Once, as in the darkness I lay asleep by night,
Strange things suddenly saw I in my dream;
All my dream was of monsters that came about me while I
    slept,
Devils and demons, four-horned, serpent-necked,
Fishes with bird-tails, three-legged bogies
From six eyes staring; dragons hideous,
Yet three-part human.
On rushed the foul flocks, grisly legions,
Stood round me, stretched out their arms,
Danced their hands about me, and sought to snatch me from
    my bed.
Then I cried (and in my dream
My voice was thick with anger and my words all awry),
'Ill-spawned elves, how dare you
Beset with your dire shapes Creation's cleanest

Shapeliest creature, Man?' Then straightway I struck out,
Flashed my fists like lightning among them, thumped like
   thunder,
Here slit Jack-o'-Lantern,
Here smashed fierce Hog-Face,
Battered wights and goblins,
Smote venturous vampires, pounded in the dust
Imps, gnomes and lobs,
Kobolds and kelpies;
Swiped bulge-eyed bogies, oafs and elves;
Clove Tough-head's triple skull, threw down
Clutching Night-hag, flogged the gawky Ear-wig Fiend
That floundered toward me on its tail.

I struck at staring eyes,
Stamped on upturned faces; through close ranks
Of hoofs I cut my way, buried my fingers deep
In half-formed flesh;
Ghouls tore at my touch; I slit sharp noses,
Trod on red tongues, seized shaggy manes,
Shook bald-heads by the beard.
Then was a scuffling. Arms and legs together
Chasing, crashing and sliding; a helter-skelter
Of feet lost and found in the tugging and toppling,
Cuffing, cudgelling, frenzied flogging . . .

So fought I, till terror and dismay
Shook those foul flocks; panic spread like a flame
Down mutinous ranks; they stand, they falter,
Those ghastly legions; but fleeing, suddenly turn
Glazed eyes upon me, to see how now I fare.
At last, to end their treachery
Again I rushed upon them, braved their slaver and snares,
Stood on a high place, and lashed down among them,
Shrieking and cursing as my blows crashed.

Then three by three and four by four
One after another hop-a-trot they fled,
Bellowing and bawling till the air was full of their breath—

Grumbling and snarling,
Those vanquished ogres, demons discomfited,
Some that would fain have run
Lolling and lurching, some that for cramped limbs
Could not stir from where they stood. Some over
    belly-wounds
Bent double; some in agony gasping and groaning.
Suddenly the clouds broke and (I knew not why)
A thin light filtered the darkness; then, while again
I sighed in wonder that those disastrous creatures,
Dire monstrosities, should dare assail
A clean and comely man, . . . there sounded in my ears
A twittering and crowing. And outdoors it was light.
The noisy cock, mindful that dawn was in the sky,
Had crowed his warning, and the startled ghosts,
Because they heard dawn heralded, had fled
In terror and tribulation from the rising day.

WANG YEN-SHOU
(trans. by Arthur Waley)

'Who's in the Next Room?'

'Who's in the next room?—who?
    I seemed to see
Somebody in the dawning passing through,
    Unknown to me.'
'Nay: you saw nought. He passed invisibly.'

'Who's in the next room?—who?
    I seem to hear
Somebody muttering firm in a language new
    That chills the ear.'
'No: you catch not his tongue who has entered there.'
    'Who's in the next room?—who?
        I seem to feel
His breath like a clammy draught, as if it drew
    From the Polar Wheel.'
'No: none who breathes at all does the door conceal.'

'Who's in the next room?—who?
　　A figure wan
With a message to one in there of something due?
　　Shall I know him anon?'
'Yea he; and he brought such; and you'll know him anon.'

THOMAS HARDY

The Ghost

'Who knocks?' 'I, who was beautiful,
　　Beyond all dreams to restore,
I, from the roots of the dark thorn am hither,
　　And knock on the door.'

'Who speaks?' 'I—once was my speech
　　Sweet as the bird's on the air,
When echo lurks by the waters to heed;
　　'Tis I speak thee fair.'

'Dark is the hour!' 'Ay, and cold.'
　　'Lone is my house.' 'Ah, but mine?'
'Sight, touch, lips, eyes yearned in vain.'
　　'Long dead these to thine . . .'

Silence. Still faint on the porch
　　Brake the flames of the stars.
In gloom groped a hope-wearied hand
　　Over keys, bolts, and bars.

A face peered. All the grey night
　　In chaos of vacancy shone;
Nought but vast sorrow was there—
　　The sweet cheat gone.

WALTER DE LA MARE

Green Candles

'There's someone at the door,' said gold candlestick:
'Let her in quick, let her in quick!'
'There is a small hand groping at the handle.
Why don't you turn it?' asked green candle.

'Don't go, don't go,' said the Hepplewhite chair,
'Lest you find a strange lady there.'
'Yes, stay where you are,' whispered the white wall:
'There is nobody there at all.'

'I know her little foot,' grey carpet said:
'Who but I should know her light tread?'
'She shall come in,' answered the open door,
'And not,' said the room, 'go out any more.'

HUMBERT WOLFE

The Magic Wood

The wood is full of shining eyes,
The wood is full of creeping feet,
The wood is full of tiny cries:
You must not go to the wood at night!

I met a man with eyes of glass
And a finger as curled as the wriggling worm,
And hair all red with rotting leaves,
And a stick that hissed like a summer snake.

The wood is full of shining eyes,
The wood is full of creeping feet,
The wood is full of tiny cries:
You must not go to the wood at night!

He sang me a song in backwards words,
And drew me a dragon in the air.
I saw his teeth through the back of his head,
And a rat's eyes winking from his hair.

The wood is full of shining eyes,
The wood is full of creeping feet,
The wood is full of tiny cries:
You must not go to the wood at night!

He made me a penny out of a stone,
And showed me the way to catch a lark
With a straw and a nut and a whispered word
And a pennorth of ginger wrapped up in a leaf.

The wood is full of shining eyes,
The wood is full of creeping feet,
The wood is full of tiny cries:
You must not go to the wood at night!

He asked me my name, and where I lived;
I told him a name from my Book of Tales;
He asked me to come with him into the wood
And dance with the Kings from under the hills.

The wood is full of shining eyes,
The wood is full of creeping feet,
The wood is full of tiny cries:
You must not go to the wood at night!

But I saw that his eyes were turning to fire;
I watched the nails grow on his wriggling hand;
And I said my prayers, all out in a rush,
And found myself safe on my father's land.

Oh, the wood is full of shining eyes,
The wood is full of creeping feet,
The wood is full of tiny cries:
You must not go to the wood at night!

HENRY TREECE

★ **Talking** —In small groups, spend some time talking about your dreams.

Do you dream often or only at particular times when things out of the ordinary are happening—before examinations, or when you are ill?

Are there some things which happen repeatedly in your dreams?

How do your dreams end?

Do you dream in colour or in black and white?

What role do you have most often? the hero? the villain? the bystander?

Where do the subjects of your dreams come from? Your own recent experience? Things that happened years ago? Television?

Have you ever had dreams about something that actually happened later?

What are the most vivid and frightening things about your nightmares?

★ **Writing.** Dreams are often illogical; people and places come and go without reason or explanation; and often scenes change with great rapidity—like film shots 'dissolving' quickly. When you are writing, try to capture the dream effects: do not feel you have to explain everything.

—Write a poem about your most vivid dream or nightmare. The nightmarish picture of Medusa on pp. 146–7 may set your imagination working.

—Most people daydream at one time or another and many of you will agree that school is a good place to do it! Why not put your daydreams to some use by writing about them? Start your poem in the real world: you may be at home, or school, or travelling on a bus or train with nothing to do; then let your poem wander into your dream-world until something happens to jolt you out of it.

—At some time in our lives most of us feel very frightened. Often such fears are associated with darkness. If you have experienced being gripped by fear perhaps you could write a poem about it, or about one of the following:

    walking home after dark;

    walking through woods on a windy night;

    my bedroom when it's dark;

    the feeling that someone is following me.

—Look carefully at the photograph of Salvador Dali's painting *Apparition of a Face and a Fruit Dish on a Beach* on pp. 142–3. What is dream-like about it? Are there any things which you cannot identify exactly, or which seem to change as you look at them?

Imagine yourself on the beach (*is* it a beach?) and write a poem describing what you see as you begin to walk towards the hills (*are* they hills?)

Alternatively, you could write a poem to describe your own dream-landscape where you find scenes and people strangely altered.

★ **Performing** —Three conversations . . . Three poems in this section are written as ghostly conversations and they can all be performed by two or more voices. The three are Thomas Hardy's *Who's In The Next Room?* (p. 144), Walter de la Mare's *The Ghost* (p. 145) and Humbert Wolfe's *Green Candles* (p. 146). All three need careful rehearsal (use a tape-recorder to practise) and you will have to experiment with getting the right ghostly tones.

—*The Magic Wood* (p. 147). This poem can make a powerful performance—you might choose to work on it in a drama room rather than a classroom—and can involve a large group. The hypnotic, chanted chorus can be said by the whole class or different groups of about five people can say the lines each time they appear. The main story can be given to one voice and two other people can act it out in a mime.

People

My Parents Kept Me

My parents kept me from children who were rough
Who threw words like stones and who wore torn clothes.
Their thighs showed through rags. They ran in the street
And climbed cliffs and stripped by the country streams.

I feared more than tigers their muscles like iron
Their jerking hands and their knees tight on my arms.
I feared the salt coarse pointing of those boys
Who copied my lisp behind me on the road.

They were lithe, they sprang out behind hedges
Like dogs to bark at my world. They threw mud
While I looked the other way, pretending to smile.
I longed to forgive them, but they never smiled.

STEPHEN SPENDER

Hunter Trials

It's awfully bad luck on Diana,
  Her ponies have swallowed their bits;
She fished down their throats with a spanner
  And frightened them all into fits.

So now she's attempting to borrow.
  Do lend her some bits, Mummy, *do*;
I'll lend her my own for tomorrow,
  But to-day *I'll* be wanting them too.

Just look at Prunella on Guzzle;
  The wizardest pony on earth;
Why doesn't she slacken his muzzle
  And tighten the breech in his girth?

I say, Mummy, there's Mrs Geyser
  And doesn't she look pretty sick?
I bet it's because Mona Lisa
  Was hit on the hock with a brick.

Miss Blewitt says Monica threw it,
  But Monica says it was Joan,
And Joan's very thick with Miss Blewitt,
  So Monica's sulking alone.

And Margaret failed in her paces,
  Her withers got tied in a noose,
So her coronet's caught in the traces
  And now all her fetlocks are loose.

Oh, it's me now. I'm terribly nervous.
  I wonder if Smudges will shy.
She's practically certain to swerve as
  Her Pelham is over one eye.

          *   *   *

Oh, wasn't it naughty of Smudges?
  Oh, Mummy, I'm sick with disgust.
She threw me in front of the Judges,
  And my silly old collarbone's bust.

                    JOHN BETJEMAN

Thrushes

The City Financier
walks in the gardens
stiffly, because of
his pride and his burdens.

The daisies, looking
up, observe
only a self-
respecting curve.

The thrushes only
see a flat
table-land
of shiny hat.

He looks importantly
about him,
while all the spring
goes on without him.

HUMBERT WOLFE

Roman Wall Blues

Over the heather the wet wind blows,
I've lice in my tunic and a cold in my nose.

The rain comes pattering out of the sky,
I'm a Wall soldier, I don't know why.

The mist creeps over the hard grey stone,
My girl's in Tungria; I sleep alone.

Aulus goes hanging around her place,
I don't like his manners, I don't like his face.

Piso's a Christian, he worships a fish;
There'd be no kissing if he had his wish.

She gave me a ring but I diced it away;
I want my girl and I want my pay.

When I'm a veteran with only one eye
I shall do nothing but look at the sky.

W. H. AUDEN

Useful Person

We'd missed the train. Two hours to wait
On Lime Street Station, Liverpool,
With *not a single thing to do*.
The bar was shut and Dad was blue
And Mum was getting in a state
And everybody felt a fool.
Yes, we were very glum indeed.
Myself, I'd nothing new to read,
No sweets to eat, no game to play.
'I'm bored,' I said, and straight away,
Mum said what I knew she'd say:
'Go on, then, read a book, OK?'
'I've *read* them *both*!' 'That's no excuse.'

Dad sat sighing, *'What* a day . . .
This is precious little use.
I wish they'd open up that bar.'
They didn't, though. No way.

And everybody else was sitting
In that waiting-room and knitting,
Staring, scratching, yawning, smoking.
'All right, Dad?' 'You must be joking!
This is precious little use.
It's like a prison. Turn me loose!'

('Big fool, act your age!' Mum hisses.
'Sorry, missus.'
'Worse than him, you are,' said Mum.)

It was grim. It was glum.

And then the Mongol child came up,
Funny-faced:
Something in her body wrong,
Something in her mind
Misplaced:

Something in her eyes was strange:
What, or why, I couldn't tell:
But somehow she was beautiful
As well.

Anyway, she took us over!
'Hello, love,' said Dad. She said,
'*There*, sit *there*!' and punched a spot
On the seat. The spot was what,
Almost, Mum was sitting on,
So Dad squeezed up, and head-to-head,
And crushed-up, hip-to-hip, they sat.
'What next, then?' 'Kiss!' 'Oh no, not that!'
Dad said, chuckling. '*Kiss!*'
                                    They did!

I thought my Mum would flip her lid
With laughing. Then the Mongol child
Was filled with pleasure—she went wild,
Running round the tables, telling
Everyone to *kiss* and yelling
Out to everyone to sit
Where she said. They did, too. It
Was sudden happiness because
The Mongol child
Was what she was:
Bossy, happy, full of fun,
And just *determined* everyone
Should have a good time too! We knew
That's what we'd got to do.

Goodness me, she took us over!
All the passengers for Dover,
Wolverhampton, London, Crewe—
Everyone from everywhere
Began to share
Her point of view! The more they squeezed,
And laughed, and fooled about, the more
The Mongol child
Was pleased!

Dad had to kiss another Dad
('Watch it, lad!' '*You* watch it, lad!'
'Stop: you're not my kind of bloke!')
Laugh? I thought that Mum would choke!

And so the time whirled by. The train
Whizzed us home again
And on the way I thought of her:
Precious little use is what
Things had been. Then she came
And things were not
The same!

She was precious, she was little,
She was useful too:
Made us speak when we were dumb,
Made us smile when we were blue,
Cheered us up when we were glum,
Lifted us when we were flat:
Who could be
More use than that?

Mongol child,
Funny-faced,
Something in your body wrong,
Something in your mind
Misplaced,
Something in your eyes, strange:
What, or why, I cannot tell:
I thought you were beautiful:

Useful, as well.

KIT WRIGHT

A Piece of Sky

There was this child,
Not very old,
Who looked at the sky
Blue pink and gold
And wanted a piece,
Just a pie-sized slice,
To hold.
He knew just how it would feel.
Treasure heavy it would weigh
And magic, it would change colour
With the day
From light to dark, from blue to grey.
He didn't want to keep it,
Just to borrow,
They could put it back again,
He said,
Tomorrow.
They questioned him with what and why.
The sky,
He said
Was like a dome that fitted the earth
Exactly half-way down.
It drew the horizon,
Outlined the trees,
Held down the mountains
And stemmed the seas.
And the tide?
Too many people on one side
Of the world,
East or West, South or North,
Tilted it and made the seas slop back and forth.
And cloud?
Cloud was fog on holiday.
And fog?
Fog was cloud, the other way.
And rainbows?
Rainbows were the ghosts of lights

That people switched off
In the middles of nights.
And . . .?
He tired of questions
He was ready for bed
He didn't know everything he said.
Their questions really made him sigh
All he had wanted was a piece of sky.
They explained the world to him.
Told him the what and where and why
Of cloud and rainbows, sky and tide
Until he thought his brains were fried.
Then he smiled at them, politely sceptic
After all, their explanation of the world
Was too fantastic.

JULIE HOLDER

Going Through the Old Photos

Me, my dad
and my brother
we were looking through the old photos.
Pictures of my dad with a broken leg
and my mum with big flappy shorts on
and me on a tricycle
when we got to one of my mum
with a baby on her knee,
and I go,
'Is that me or Brian?'
And my dad says,
'Let's have a look.
It isn't you or Brian,' he says.
'It's Alan.
He died.
He would have been
two years younger than Brian
and two years older than you.
He was a lovely baby.'

'How did he die?'
'Whooping cough.
I was away at the time.
He coughed himself to death in Connie's arms.
The terrible thing is,
it wouldn't happen today,
but it was during the war, you see,
and they didn't have the medicines.
That must be the only photo
of him we've got.'

Me and Brian
looked at the photo.
We couldn't say anything.
It was the first time we had ever heard about Alan.
For a moment I felt ashamed
like as if I had done something wrong.

I looked at the baby trying to work out
who he looked like.
I wanted to know what another brother
would have been like.
No way of saying.
And Mum looked so happy.
Of course she didn't know
when they took the photo
that he would die, did she?

Funny thing is,
though my father mentioned it every now and then
over the years,
Mum—never.
And he never said anything in front of her
about it
and we never let on that we knew.
What I've never figured out
was whether
her silence was because
she was more upset about it
than my dad—
or less.

MICHAEL ROSEN

Rodge said,

'Teachers—they want it all ways—
You're jumping up and down on a chair
or something
and they grab hold of you and say,
"Would you do that sort of thing in your own home?"

'So you say, "No."
And they say,
"Well don't do it here then."

'But if you say, "Yes, I do it at home."
they say,
"Well, we don't want that sort of thing
going on here
thank you very much."

'Teachers—they get you all ways,'
Rodge said.

MICHAEL ROSEN

★ **Performing** —*Hunter Trials* by John Betjeman (p. 154) needs to be read in an exaggeratedly upper-class accent. It's really written to be read by one voice but with a bit of thought you could split it up between two or three if you preferred.

—*Useful Person* by Kit Wright (p. 158) can be read with different people taking the part of narrator (boy), Mum, Dad, the other man on the train and, of course, the little mongol girl. (What used to be called mongolism is usually called 'Down's syndrome' these days. 'Down's babies' never fully grow up mentally and are often very beautiful.) It's a poem to make you think and needs careful reading.

—*Rodge said* (p. 165) can be performed with three voices. One simply says 'Rodge said' at the beginning and end of the poem; one takes the part of Rodge and one is the teacher. Try to get the aggrieved tone of Rodge's voice and the rather bossy voice of the teacher.

★ **Writing.** Have you ever been on a bus or train or in a queue surrounded by people you don't know and wondered who they are, where they live and what they do? If you are regularly in this situation—travelling to and from school, for example—think about the people you see and jot down the things that strike you. Try to organise your ideas into a poem.

—When people are older they may not be able to get about much. The front window may become their only window on to the world where they can see life pass by. If you know such a person, either write a poem to describe him or her, or one which sets down what you imagine to be the stream of thoughts, feelings and memories going through the person's mind.

—Michael Rosen's poem *Rodge said* is about the way teachers always seem to win. It's not just teachers who 'get you all ways', though. Brothers and sisters and parents seem to 'win' as well. Write a different version of the poem about this. You could start 'Brothers (or 'parents', or 'sisters')—they want it all ways—' and then go on to say what you're complaining about.

Town and Country

Cycling Down the Street to Meet my Friend John

On my bike and down our street,
Swinging round the bend,
Whizzing past the Library,
Going to meet my friend.

Silver flash of spinning spokes,
Whirr of oily chain,
Bump of tyre on railway line
Just before the train.

The road bends sharp at Pinfold Lane
Like a broken arm,
Brush the branches of the trees
Skirting Batty's Farm.

Tread and gasp and strain and bend
Climbing Gallows' Slope,
Flying down the other side
Like an antelope.

Swanking into Johnnie's street,
Cycling hands on hips,
Past O'Connors corner shop
That always smells of chips.

Bump the door of his back-yard
Where we always play,
Lean my bike and knock the door,
'Can John come out to play?'

GARETH OWEN

George Square

George Square
idleness
an island
children splashing
in a sea of pigeons
pigeons strutting
pigeon-toed.

And we
city dwellers
sitting
separate
close together.
City dwellers
we only know
nature captive—
zoos and gardens
Latin-tagged.
We know no earth
or roots.
We see no slow
season shift
but sudden summer
blaze a concrete day
and catch us unawares.
We can find no sense
in traffic lights'
continual change of emphasis.

Nature captive:
this is a city
nature's barred.
But the flowers
bound and bedded
bloom
incurable as cancer
and as for fat old ladies'
flowery
summer dresses
my god, they really are
a riot.

LIZ LOCHHEAD

Sitting on Trev's back wall on the last day of the holidays trying to think of something to do

We sit and squint on Trev's back wall
By the clothes line
Watching the shirts flap
Hearing the shirts slap
In the sunshine.
There's nothing much to do at all
But try to keep cool
And it's our last day
Of the holiday
Tomorrow we're back at school.

We keep suggesting games to play
Like Monopoly,
But you need a day
If you want to play
It properly.
We played for four hours yesterday
Between rainfalls
In Trev's front room
That's like a tomb
And always smells of mothballs.

Says Trev, 'Why don't we kick a ball
Over the Wasteground?'
But the weather's got
Far too hot
To run around.
John kicks his heels against the wall
Stokesy scratches his head
I head a ball
Chalk my name on the wall
While Trev pretends that he's dead.

Says John, 'Let's go to the cinder track
And play speedway.
We can go by the dykes
It's not far on our bikes
I'll lead the way.'
'My saddlebag's all straw at the back
Being used by blackbirds.'
'And there's something unreal
About my fixed wheel
It only drives me backwards.'

Trev's Granny chucks out crusts of bread
For the sparrows
While their black cat
Crouches flat
Winking in the shadows.
Trev leaps up and bangs his head
With a sudden roar.
'We could er . . .,' he says.
'We could er . . .,' he says.
And then sits down once more.
'Let's play Releevo on the sands,'
Says John at last.
We set out with a shout
But his mother calls out,
'It's gone half-past
Your tea's all laid, you wash your hands
They're absolutely grey.'
'Oh go on Mum
Do I have to come
We were just going out to play.'

Old Stokes trails home and pulls a face,
'I'll see you Trev.'
'See you John.'
'See you Trev.'

'See you tonight the usual place.'
'Yes right, all right.'
'Don't forget.'
'You bet.'
'See you then tonight.'
'See you.'
'See you.'
'See
You.'

GARETH OWEN

Summer Night

As we walk, the moon ahead of us
Appears to be falling through
Each tree we pass, and sieves
Star after star through screens
Of thickening leaves.

The green hedge is wider now
With white may, hanging grass. The chestnut
Trims itself with pink and snowy cones;
The moon as we walk drops through each tree
And scatters silvery grit among the country stones.

JAMES KIRKUP

The Winter Trees

Against the evening sky the trees are black,
Iron themselves against the iron rails;
The hurrying crowds seek cinemas or homes,
A cosy hour where warmth will mock the wind.
They do not look at the trees now summer's gone,
For fallen with the leaves are those glad days
Of sand and sea and ships, of swallows, lambs,
Of cricket teams, and walking long in woods.

Standing among the trees a shadow bends
And picks a cigarette-end from the ground;
It lifts the collar of an overcoat,
And blows upon its hands and stamps its feet—
For this is winter, chastiser of the free,
This is the winter, kind only to the bound.

CLIFFORD DYMENT

I Know Some Lonely Houses off the Road

I know some lonely houses off the road
A robber'd like the look of,—
Wooden barred,
And windows hanging low,
Inviting to
A portico,

Where two could creep:
One hand the tools,
The other peep
To make sure all's asleep.
Old-fashioned eyes,
Not easy to surprise!

How orderly the kitchen'd look by night,
With just a clock,—
But they could gag the tick,
And mice won't bark;
And so the walls don't tell,
None will.

A pair of spectacles ajar just stir—
An almanac's aware.
Was it the mat winked,
Or a nervous star?
The moon slides down the stair
To see who's there.

There's plunder,—where?
Tankard, or spoon,
Earring, or stone,
A watch, some ancient brooch
To match the grandmamma,
Staid sleeping there.

Day rattles, too,
Stealth's slow;
The sun has got as far
As the third sycamore.
Screams chanticleer,
'Who's there?'

And echoes, trains away,
Sneer—'Where?'
While the old couple, just astir,
Think that the sunrise left the door ajar!

EMILY DICKINSON

Fishing Harbour towards Evening

Slashed clouds leak gold. Along the slurping wharf
The snugged boats creak and seesaw. Round the masts

Abrasive squalls flake seagulls off the sky:
Choppy with wings the rapids of shrill sound.

Wrapt in spliced airs of fish and tar,
Light wincing on their knives, the clockwork men

Incise and scoop the oily pouches, flip
The soft guts overboard with blood-wet fingers.

Among three rhythms the slapping silver turns
To polished icy marble upon the deck.

RICHARD KELL

The Beech

Strength leaves the hand I lay on this beech-bole
    So great-girthed, old and high;
Its sprawling arms like iron serpents roll
    Between me and the sky.

One elbow on the sloping earth it leans,
    That steeply falls beneath,
As though resting a century it means
    To take a moment's breath.

Its long thin buds in glistering varnish dipt
    Are swinging up and down
While one young beech that winter left unstript
    Still wears its withered crown.

At least gust of the wind the great tree heaves
    From heavy twigs to groin;
The wind sighs as it rakes among dead leaves
    For some lost key or coin.

And my blood shivers as away it sweeps
    Rustling the leaves that cling
Too late to that young withered beech that keeps
    Its autumn in the spring.

ANDREW YOUNG

Throwing a Tree

The two executioners stalk along over the knolls,
Bearing two axes with heavy heads shining and wide,
And a long limp two-handled saw toothed for cutting great
    boles,
And so they approach the proud tree that bears the
    death-mark on its side.

Jackets doffed they swing axes and chop away just above
    ground,
And the chips fly about and lie white on the moss and fallen
    leaves;
Till a broad deep gash in the bark is hewn all the way round,
And one of them tries to hook upward a rope, which at last
    he achieves.

The saw then begins, till the top of the tall giant shivers:
The shivers are seen to grow greater each cut than before:
They edge out the saw, tug the rope; but the tree only
    quivers,
And kneeling and sawing again, they step back to try pulling
    once more.

Then, lastly, the living mast sways, further sways: with a
    shout
Job and Ike rush aside. Reached the end of its long staying
    powers
The tree crashes downward: it shakes all its neighbours
    throughout,
And two hundred years' steady growth has been ended in
    less than two hours.

THOMAS HARDY

Root Cellar

Nothing would sleep in that cellar, dank as a ditch,
Bulbs broke out of boxes hunting for chinks in the dark,
Shoots dangled and drooped,
Lolling obscenely from mildewed crates,
Hung down long yellow evil necks, like tropical
    snakes.
And what a congress of stinks!—
Roots ripe as old bait,
Pulpy stems, rank, silo-rich,
Leaf-mould, manure, lime, piled against slippery
    planks.
Nothing would give up life:
Even the dirt kept breathing a small breath.

THEODORE ROETHKE

Digging

Today I think
Only with scents—scents dead leaves yield,
And bracken, and wild carrot's seed,
And the square mustard field;

Odours that rise
When the spade wounds the root of tree,
Rose, currant, raspberry, or goutweed,
Rhubarb or celery;

The smoke's smell, too,
Flowing from where a bonfire burns
The dead, the waste, the dangerous,
And all to sweetness turns.

It is enough
To smell, to crumble the dark earth,
While the robin sings over again
Sad songs of Autumn mirth.

EDWARD THOMAS

In a Sailplane

Still as a bird
Transfixed in flight
We shiver and flow
Into leagues of light.

Rising and turning
Without a sound
As summer lifts us
Off the ground.

The sky's deep bell
Of glass rings down.
We slip in a sea
That cannot drown.

We kick the wide
Horizon's blues
Like a cluttering hoop
From round our shoes.

This easy 'plane
So quietly speaks,
Like a tree it sighs
In silvery shrieks.

Neatly we soar
Through a roaring cloud:
Its caverns of snow
Are dark and loud.

Into banks of sun
Above the drifts
Of quilted cloud
Our stillness shifts.

Here no curious
Bird comes near.
We float alone
In a snowman's sphere.

Higher than spires
Where breath is rare
We beat the shires
Of racing air.

Up the cliff
Of sheer no-place
We swarm a rope
That swings on space.

Breezed by a star's
Protracted stare
We watch the earth
Drop out of air.

Red stars of light
Burn on the round
Of land: street-constellations
Strew the ground.

Their bridges leap
From town to town:
Into lighted dusk
We circle down.

Still as a bird
Transfixed in flight
We come to nest
In the field of night.

JAMES KIRKUP

★ **Performing** —*Cycling Down the Street* (p. 167) and *I Know Some Lonely Houses* (p. 173) are both best spoken by single voices; but they are quite different. Practise your readings. Try to catch the changes in mood and energy in the cycle ride and the feeling of stealth in the imaginary burglary in the second poem.

—*George Square* (p. 168). One reader could take the first and last sections. The longer middle section could be spoken by five 'city dwellers' taking a sentence each.

—*Sitting on Trev's back wall* (p. 170). A group of five could work on a reading, live or taped. You will need a narrator and the voices of Trev, John, Stokesy and John's Mum. Work out who says which lines carefully and rehearse your performance.

—Names. Look at all the names in *Cycling Down the Street* (p. 167)—buildings, roads, shops . . . Think of your own area and list as many place names as you can; some may be official signs, others may just be the way you and your friends refer to places. Begin each line with a place name from your list. Complete each line with a few words to bring the place alive for your reader.

★ **Notebook** —L. S. Lowry's picture of a busy market-place may remind you of a similar scene in your own town or place you visit. Next time you go there take a notebook with you and try to see with a writer's eye. Jot down things that strike you such as colours, sounds, smells; try to capture the movement and bustle, the *life* of the place. From your jottings try to write a poem which will re-create for your reader the sense of actually being there. If you can't make an actual visit, try to think yourself into Lowry's picture and draw on your memories of busy market scenes to make it come alive.

Acknowledgments

The editors and publishers would like to thank the following for their kind permission to reproduce copyright material:

John Agard: 'Woodpecker' from *I Like that Stuff* (Cambridge University Press): 'Limbo Dancer's Mantra' from *Mangoes and Bullets* (Pluto Press). Both by permission of John Agard.

G. Apollinaire: 'Calligram' from *Selected Poems*, Penguin Books Ltd.

W. H. Auden: 'The Quarry' and 'Roman Wall Blues' from *Collected Shorter Poems 1927–1957*, Faber & Faber Ltd.

Hilaire Belloc: 'Tarantella', reprinted by permission of A. D. Peters & Co.

Francis Berry: 'Fall of a Tower' from *The Galloping Centaur*, Methuen & Co. Ltd.

Alan Brownjohn: 'The Rabbit'.

John Betjeman: 'Hunter Trials' from *Collected Poems*, Macmillan.

Edward Kamau Braithwaite: 'Limbo' © Oxford University Press 1973. Reprinted from *The Arrivants* by Edward Kamau Brathwaite (1973) by permission of Oxford University Press; 'Cat' © Oxford University Press 1975. Reprinted from *Other Exiles* by Edward Kamau Brathwaite (1975) by permission of Oxford University Press.

Charles Causley: 'Ballad of the Bread Man' from *Collected Poems 1951–75*, Macmillan Publishers and David Higham Associates Ltd.

Tony Connor: 'Child's Bouncing Song'.

John Cotton: 'In the Kitchen' © John Cotton 1985. Reprinted from *The Crystal Zoo*: poems by John Cotton, L. J. Anderson and U. A. Fanthorpe (1985) by permission of Oxford University Press

e. e. cummings: 'Insu nli gh t' and 'One' from *73 Poems* by e. e. cummings, © 1963 by Marion Morehouse Cummings. Reprinted by permission of Harcourt Brace & World Inc., and MacGibbon & Kee; 'In Just-spring', copyright 1923, 1951, by e. e. cummings. Reprinted by permission of Harcourt, Brace & World Inc., and MacGibbon & Kee; 'r-p-o-p-h-e-s-s-a-g-r' from *Complete Poems 1913–1962*, Grafton Books.

Emily Dickinson: 'I Started Early' reprinted by permission of the publishers and the Trustees of Amherst College from Thomas H. Johnson, Editor, *The Poems of Emily Dickinson*, Cambridge, Mass., U.S.A.: The Belknap Press of Harvard University Press, copyright 1951, 1955, by the President and Fellows of Harvard College.

Kevin Dickson: 'Guitar', Wandsworth School.

Clifford Dyment: 'Carrion' and 'Winter Trees' from *Poems 1935–1948*, J. M. Dent & Sons Ltd.

Marriott Edgar and Stanley Holloway: 'The Lion and Albert', Methuen Children's Books.

T. S. Eliot: 'Skimbleshanks: The Railway Cat' from *Old Possum's Book of Practical Cats*, Faber & Faber Ltd.

Eleanor Farjeon: 'Mrs Malone' and 'Cat!' from *Silver Sand and Snow*, published by Michael Joseph, by permission of David Higham Associates Ltd and The Estate of Eleanor Farjeon; 'Cats' from *The Children's Bells* by Eleanor Farjeon, Oxford University Press.

Lawrence Ferlinghetti: 'Johnny Nolan' from *A Coney Island of the Mind*, © 1958 by Lawrence Ferlinghetti. Reprinted by permission of Laurence Pollinger Ltd, and New Directions Publishing Corporation, New York.

Rachel Field: 'Meeting' from *Poems for Children*, William Heinemann Ltd.

David Gascoyne: 'The Very Image' from *Collected Poems*, Oxford University Press, and 'Vista'.

Harry Graham: 'Tender-Heartedness', 'The Stern Parent' and 'Appreciation' from *Ruthless Rhymes for Heartless Homes*, Edward Arnold (Publishers) Ltd.

Thomas Hardy: 'Silences', 'Who's in the Next Room?' and 'Throwing a Tree' from *The Collected Poems of Thomas Hardy*, the Trustees of the Hardy Estate, Macmillan & Co. Ltd, and the Macmillan Company of Canada.

John Heath-Stubbs: 'The Gecko' from *Collected Poems*, Oxford University Press.

Phoebe Hesketh: 'The Heron' from *Prayer for the Sun*, Oxford University Press.

John Hillelson: *North American Train*, © 1875 by permission of the John Hillelson Collection.

Julie Holder: 'A Piece of Sky' from *A Third Poetry Book*, compiled by John Foster, Oxford University Press.

G. M. Hopkins: 'Inversnaid' from *Collected Poems*, Oxford University Press.

Ted Hughes: 'The Jaguar' from *The Hawk in the Rain*, Faber & Faber Ltd, and Harper & Row, Inc., New York; 'Woodpecker' from *Under the North Star*, Faber and Faber Ltd.

Richard Kell: 'Pigeons' from *Control Tower*, Chatto & Windus Ltd.

James Kirkup: 'Thunder and Lightning', 'Early Rain', 'In a Sailplane' and 'Summer Night' from *The Prodigal Son*, Oxford University Press.

D. H. Lawrence: 'Mountain Lion', 'Two Performing Elephants' and 'Storm in the Black Forest' from *The Complete Poems of D. H. Lawrence*, Laurence Pollinger Ltd, and the Estate of the late Mrs Frieda Lawrence.

Denise Levertov: 'The Disclosure' from *O Taste and See*, © by Denise Levertov Goodman, and reprinted by permission of New Directions Publishing Corporation, New York.

Vachel Lindsay: 'The Sea Serpent Chantey' from *Collected Poems*, Macmillan.

Homework- Describe how you created your
time-table- NOTE FORMAT.

from beginning-

NOTE FORMAT.

N.B
pointing

Draw Print window,

Copies 1   Pages All